Your Fortune in Foreclosures

Your Fortune in Foreclosures

Today's Best, Low-Risk, High-Profit
Real Estate Investment

Fredy Bush,
Carl Hunter
& Bruce Erb

K

Knight-Ridder Press
Tucson, Arizona

Published by Knight-Ridder Press
A division of HPBooks, Inc.
P.O. Box 5367
Tucson, Arizona 85703

Printed in U.S.A.
9 8 7 6 5 4 3 2
1st Printing

Library of Congress Cataloging in Publication Data

Bush, Loretta Fredy
  Your fortune in foreclosures

  Includes index.
  1. Real estate investment. 2. House buying.
3. Foreclosure. 4. Real property. I. Hunter, Carl.
II. Title.
HDL382.5.B87 1987   332.63'24   86-33793
ISBN 0-89586-572-6

7134971

Contents

Foreword

It has been only a few years now since we, Fredy Bush and Carl Hunter, attended a real estate seminar. You might have attended a similar seminar yourself, where speakers offer to teach you the secrets of creating a lifetime of wealth through real estate investment. Many of these seminars do in fact teach investing methods that work. Hundreds of real estate millionaires have real estate seminars to thank for pointing them in the right direction.

One such speaker caught our attention. He convinced us that there was a fortune to be made by investing in property that was in foreclosure. Owners of such property, we were told, will practically give their homes away—and thank investors for their kindness in buying them for pennies on the dollar.

Unfortunately, reality—that breaker of dreams—treated us to a rude awakening. Owners in trouble are rarely happy to meet investors. In fact, many owners, when faced with the nightmare of foreclosure, quickly develop an attitude of, "If I can't keep my home, I'll make sure that you don't get it either!"

Although at first we were disappointed, we remained determined. And we found some solutions. We discovered a way to make money—lots of money—from properties facing foreclosure. We make it in a way that allows the owners to walk away smiling. How much money, you wonder? Well, on our first deal we put $20,000 in our pockets with less than one month's effort. We'll take a close look at that particular transaction later in this book, and by then you'll know that a profit of such magnitude is not impossible.

Of course, we continued to buy foreclosure properties, but the more we worked in foreclosures the more we discovered widespread ignorance on the subject. Homeowners, bankers, title officers, real estate agents—just about everyone involved—were working in the dark. It was staggering how many real estate "experts" knew almost nothing about the foreclosure process.

To combat the general lack of knowledge we formed a company, called it "Fortune Businesses," and began teaching seminars of our own. We didn't teach investors how to exploit desperate owners. Our approach is to show investors, real estate professionals, and homeowners in trouble how to avoid the embarrassing and costly fiasco called foreclosure.

Our efforts were lauded by those who attended, but we wanted to reach a wider audience and teach what we had learned by hard experience: that foreclosures can be avoided, and everyone—from the seller to the banker to the buyer—can come out ahead.

This book is the result of that desire.

If you have ever or will ever own real estate, this book is for you. If you will ever have anything to do with real estate in any professional capacity, this book is also for you. If you want to invest your time, effort, and money in anything at all, to achieve your financial goals, this book is for you. We sincerely hope and believe that you'll profit from what we've written, whether you are an investor, professional or homeowner.

When you read this book, you'll notice that we've tried to make it as personal as possible—from us to you. We're not big on formality, and, to be honest, we don't like boring business books any more than you do. That's why we've filled it with personal experiences and tried to write everything in plain, readable English.

The hardest part about writing it, we found out, is in how to narrate our stories. So throughout the book you'll find a lot of the word "we." Occasionally you'll run across a "Carl did this . . ." or a "Fredy did that . . ." but for the most part it will be "we found that . . ." meaning both of us. Clear enough?

A warm thank you goes to our colleague Bruce Erb for keeping the "we's" in line.

An American Nightmare

Midnight had come and gone long before Paul finally gave up and went to bed. And even after he had given into his exhaustion and lay down, sleep was a long time in coming. His mind raced round and round, like a fox in a cage trying to catch its own tail. He listened to Vicky's peaceful breathing for what seemed like hours, and the pain, shame and anger flared up viciously.

It just wasn't fair, he thought. He had worked hard— damned hard, for years and years, giving up practically everything fun—and for what? Laid off! How could they have laid him off? He was the best foreman!

This was his home; his castle. They were going to take away the only thing he'd ever owned that was worth anything. Jenny and Renee were in school; they had friends. How do you tell your little girls that daddy lost the house; that they were going to be leaving their home to live in a tiny apartment . . . .

And Vicky. Of course she could sleep. She just *knew* he would figure something out. Well, guess what, Vicky; guess what? Your dear, dependable, loving Paul really did it this time. He went and got himself laid off, and nobody is hiring, and the bills haven't been paid for two months now and things are getting very sticky and who knows what will happen next, because somebody is going to take our home away from us and kick us out into the street.

He hadn't said anything yet—how could he? Every time he reread the letter from the bank in his mind, the cold sweat would break out on his brow and the shaking—somewhere deep inside, where true fear makes its home—would begin again.

In a panicky internal voice he tried to reassure himself that things would somehow work out . . . they *had* to work out. He would get a job offer; the bank would call and give him an extra month to come up with the money; some mysterious uncle that he'd never heard of would die and leave him a million dollars. And every time he listened to the voice and began to build up a wall of reassurance, an icy wind of logic would tear it down again, leaving him gasping.

He was watching his own personal American Dream turn into a nightmare.

Guess, just guess how many times the same scene is acted out in cold, dark houses across the nation. Guess how many people lose their homes? How many foreclosures occur each day across the U.S., and how many owners are left with nothing to show for years of effort but a few personal belongings and seven years of bad credit? Guess.

Would you believe over 400 every week . . . in Los Angeles alone?

Here's the punchline: It doesn't have to happen! In most cases one person—anyone, including you—could prevent the tragedy. And you can make money doing it!

This is an important, serious book, filled with as much information as any real estate book we've ever seen. By the time you've finished it you will know more about the foreclo-sure process than 80 percent of all real estate agents in the country. And if you've followed our methods and advice well enough, by the time you reach the last page you'll be ready for the ultimate test—making your own fortune in foreclosures.

We must admit here that the title is a bit misleading because the emphasis of this book is on making your fortune by *preventing* foreclosures, not by encouraging them. As you will learn, people like Paul are waiting for you. If they get a call from you, or a letter, or a personal visit, you may be able to turn their lives around and give them hope.

If the idea sounds as exciting and profitable to you as it has been for us, turn the page and let's get started.

CHAPTER ONE

Why You Should Invest In Foreclosures

For that matter, why invest at all? What's wrong with *working* for a living? Nothing. Nothing at all. In fact, investing in foreclosures, as you will find out, *is* work. It's simply very rewarding work.

ARE YOU AN INVESTOR?

Everyone is an investor, from a three-year-old boy in Detroit watching "Sesame Street" to an eighty-year-old woman in Russia milking her cow. Investing, as we'll use the term throughout the book, is merely the means by which we achieve our goals. The child wants to be entertained; he therefore invests an hour of his time, energy, and attention into watching Bert and Ernie count to five over and over again. The woman in Russia wants to have milk with which to make yogurt; to get the milk she must invest a little time and physical effort with Bossienik. Both of them are satisfying their short-range goals by investing.

You have goals, don't you? Financial, personal, spiritual, educational, and a thousand others. To achieve those goals you're going to have to invest something, whether it's time, money, talent, or another resource. And every investment means sacrifice; you will give up some goals in favor of others. If a particular goal offers enough reward—with a low enough risk of failure—to make the investment worthwhile, you will achieve that goal.

Just about everything you do, from the minute you struggle out of bed in the morning until you collapse back into it at night, is done with a goal in mind. You only have so many resources to work with: only twenty-four hours, only so much money, intelligence, charm, and good looks to get you where you want to go. And every choice you make is a choice between investments.

All we're trying to do here is get you thinking along the right lines—catching the vision of what it means to invest. If you grasp the concept, it's enough to build on. Understand this point before we move on: You have goals—short range, long range, and in-between range. To reach those goals you must invest one or more of the resources you have to draw on. You *are* an investor, like it or not.

We could easily get carried away discussing life planning and goal setting, and it would be a couple of hundred pages before we got to the heart of the book. But we're not going to get pulled off track. Of the many goals you have for yourself and your family, we're going to concentrate on only one—money.

FINANCIAL INVESTING

Like all of your goals, those that have to do with dollars will be somewhere between super short term and very long term and, if you're a member of the un-self-disciplined majority, they will lessen in definition as they get further away. Your financial goal for this week may be to make enough money to pay the bills; your lifetime goal is probably to reach the point where you're "really" rich. And that's a fine goal. A little vague, but workable for our purposes.

Okay, so let's assume you know your financial goals, or at least are making some soon. Now what? Well, now it's time to make the necessary investment of resources to achieve them. Most Americans try to reach their financial goals by investing 40 hours of their lives every week working for someone else. The return on their investment, supplied by that someone, may include job security, a pension plan, health insurance, prestige, limited power—and, of course, a paycheck. And those rewards will satisfy the financial goal of surviving as a member of the working class. The bills will get paid sooner or later; there will be a couple of economy cars in the garage and a color TV in the den.

But what if your long-range goal was to be really rich?

What you have to do is find an alternative source of money that will reward your investment to the tune of a hundred thousand or more a year. What you're looking for is a very high return on your investment. And you won't find that kind of return working for someone else.

Face it, if you want to achieve your long-range financial goals, you're going to have to invest in the big league. That means stocks and bonds, precious metals, real estate, oil, antiques, or unfriendly takeovers of large corporations.

And while you're choosing your investment you'd better take into account both risk and return. A savings account offers low risk *and* low return. (How many savings-account millionaires do you know?) You can trade commodity futures, where risk and possible return are both high, but you'd better keep the medicine cabinet well-stocked with antacids.

The actual return for most "high-return" investments is as dependable as a $5 digital watch.

THE BEST INVESTMENT

If you want a combination of high return and low risk in an investment that doesn't require a million dollars starting capital, nothing beats real estate. Nothing ever will. Real estate, when purchased carefully, is as safe and secure as the savings account. At the same time, the return can far surpass anything that commodity futures can offer.

The potential rate of return on your real estate investments is close to unbelievable. If you're not convinced, chew on this fact for a minute: more millionaires made their fortunes in real estate than in all other investments combined.

If you've ever heard of an investor who lost his or her shirt in real estate, you've heard about an investor who took an unnecessary risk. The investor bought property that, for one reason or another, was worth less when it was sold than when it was bought. And that's inexcusable. Any successful real estate investor will tell you that risk in real estate investments can be controlled.

The secret to making tons of money is as follows: Buy low; sell high.

To expand on the idea: If you want to eliminate risk and increase profit, buy property far below market value and then sell it only slightly below market value. For example, if the current market value of a home is $80,000, and you can buy it for $40,000, you should be able to sell it for $60,000 without any trouble, right? And that means $20,000 profit.

Okay, you say, now comes the rub: How am I supposed to buy a property worth $80,000 for only $40,000? I didn't just sprout up under a cabbage leaf, you know. If the house is worth $80,000, who's going to sell it to me for half that?

Calm down. We're not trying to con you. The truth is, you *can* buy property for half its market value—if you know where to look, and if you're patient. Finding those one-in-ten-thousand perfect deals is like fishing in an ocean with only a dozen whales; if you want to succeed you've got to put a lot of lines in the water and then wait for a bite. You may wait a long time, but when the right one comes along, it will be a winner.

Keeping the metaphor alive, you'll see in a moment that the ocean is presently overstocked with whoppers, and more are pouring in all the time. This is by far the best time in the history of the nation to be fishing for real estate deals.

There are as many ways to invest in real estate as there are Munchkins in Oz. But, as you can tell from the title of this book, we think foreclosures is the best way.

Why foreclosures? To answer that question, we'll discuss a few different methods for investing in real estate and then narrow down the field to the best approach.

INVESTING STRATEGIES

Historically, real estate investors have played three games: the quick buy/sell; the mid-term buy/rent/sell; and the long-term buy/don't-sell-until-you-die.

Each has its distinct advantages and disadvantages, and it's necessary to discuss each.

Buy/Sell

The first, quick buy/sell, is the toughest. It's a hard game to play, not unlike hanging out in a hundred singles bars looking for Mr. or Ms. Right. It means waiting for the perfect property to come along. This strategy will only work if you can find properties selling far below market value that can be bought, fixed up (if necessary) and resold quickly, usually in a matter of weeks.

On the good side, it can mean quick and easy profits. It's not unheard of for a quick-sell investment to net $20,000 or more in a couple of weeks. Second, it avoids the hassles of ownership and tenant management. And third, it gives your money more "turns" to the buck. In other words, would you rather make a nickel on your investment dollar once a year or ten times that? If you can turn the same profit more times per year, you'll make more money. (See how easy all of this is?)

On the bad side, those perfect deals are as rare as polar bears in the desert. Also, they require a quick and fearless mind. When the persistent investor does finally find the deal, he or she must move in quickly.

Let's look at such an investment: Judy Buyer finds a house for sale. Not just any house—this is a great little three bedroom with a white picket fence, in good condition, worth maybe $65,000. And Judy can buy this little house for only $38,500. What's the catch? No catch, really. The owners are in the middle of a messy divorce. They both want out, and they want out *now*. They haven't made a house payment in four months and the tone of voice in the letters from the bank is getting downright unfriendly. They owe $35,000 and they are desperate. The day Judy hears about the house is the first day the owners put it on the market, and she quickly moves in for the deal.

She buys the house, paying all closing costs and giving the sellers $2,000 walking money. She then lists the house with a broker and sells it for $50,000—less than a week after buying it. She nets almost $10,000, of which she'll have to give nearly a third to the tax man.

Buy/Rent/Sell

The next method is a mid-range investment that includes buying a property below market value, fixing it up, renting it out for six months or more, and then selling at a profit. For the last decade or so it's been by far the most popular investment strategy, and with good reason. It combined the best of real estate's advantages: tax savings, equity growth, appreciation, and cash flow.

The good points include a less restricted choice of properties, slightly less risk, and more after-tax profits. The dangers include vacancies, which mean negative cash flow—an "alligator" in real estate lingo; dependency on future economic trends; management hassles, such as mopping up overflowing toilets and other assorted joys that only property managers know; and the fact that the investor's money is tied up in the property for as long as he or she owns it.

A typical investment—up until 1987—went something like this: Joe Investor finds a three-bedroom house for sale. The lawn is nearly dead; the interior walls are a dark peanut-butter brown from about three feet to the floor; the peanut butter that missed the wall is ground into the carpet. Fixed up, the house would rent for about $550 per month and would sell for $62,000. In its current condition it's not worth more than $55,000—maybe less. The sellers are desperate (they were just transferred to Alaska and have four weeks to move) and they are willing to sell for $52,000. They work out terms that allow Joe to invest only $4,000 of his own money and still keep his payments down to $500 a month.

Joe fixes up the house for another $1,000. He rents it to a young family for $550 and keeps it for a year. At the end of the year he is able to sell for $65,000 (inflation has added about $3,000 to the value of the property). His total profit is over $13,000, of which Uncle Sam only takes about $2,500, thanks to capital gains. Actually, the IRS allows Joe to claim a depreciation expense, even though the market value of the property has actually gone up, and he ends up paying no taxes on the profit at all. In some cases he will actually get to show a paper loss on the deal greater than the profit from the sale and he can offset some of his regular income. With enough such properties he can "zero out" his income entirely and pay no income tax whatsoever, even though he may end up making $100,000 or more.

It's no wonder this strategy was so popular. And with all of the creative financing techniques that were dreamed up in the early 1980s, thousands of "nothing-down" investors crowded the market looking for deals exactly like the one described above.

Buy/Rent/Hold

At one time this was the most common strategy, mostly used by the wealthy to accumulate more assets for tax write-offs and long-term growth. What investment could be more rock solid than real estate?

Again, the good and the bad: The benefits include a steady cash flow, not unlike stock dividends that are paid monthly; a hedge against inflation; tax savings from depreciation; and long-term equity growth as the debt was paid down. Also, once the money borrowed to buy the property was completely paid (by the tenants), the cash flow increased dramatically.

The main disadvantages to this strategy were the same as for the last one: management worries and tied-up capital.

Since we've already set a precedent, let's take a pre-1987 case: Mary Moneymaker buys a house in excellent condition for its full market value of $75,000, putting down $12,000. Her payments on the balance are only $620, and she can rent the house for $650. After 10 years, rents have climbed to $750 and she refinances, lowering her payments to $590.

Thirty years later, when Mary is ready to retire, the loan is completely paid off. Due to inflation, she is now collecting $1,800 a month in rental income, and the house is worth $225,000.

Not a bad return on an initial $12,000 investment that has to date paid her a total of $61,200 in rental income, and will continue to pay more every year until she dies. She's had maintenance costs, of course, but she also enjoyed preferential treatment every year when tax time came around, and her tax savings more than equaled her costs.

Here's a summary of the advantages and disadvantages of each method.

Real Estate Investing

Strategy	Advantages	Disadvantages
Quick Buy/Sell	Quick profit. More "turns". Greater return on investment (usually).	Hard to find; Requires fast action. No tax breaks. No future growth.
Buy/Rent/Sell	Possible monthly income. Some tax breaks (such as depreciation). Long-term equity growth	Money is locked up. Management hassles. No guaranteed profit. Vacancy losses.
Buy/Rent/Keep	Very long-term growth. Tax advantages. Monthly income (especially after loans are paid).	Investment is tied up for years. Management problems and costs. No guaranteed appreciation.

TODAY'S MARKET

The last two strategies were great in their day. There was a time once, before we ever heard of tax reform, when those were the best games in town. Today, however, most of their advantages have been cut away. There is no such thing as capital gains. It doesn't matter whether you own the property for one day or a lifetime; you must claim all of the profit as ordinary income. Say goodbye to the incentive for holding property for more than six months.

Another advantage of holding property was depreciation expense. We had a wonderful thing called the *accelerated cost recovery system (ACRS)*, which allowed the investor to offset a great deal of income in the first years of an investment—in many cases, enough to reduce the investor's tax burden to zero. But ACRS went the way of capital gains. Now we have a 27.5-year straight-line depreciation (Translation: you don't get to offset as much income).

Even worse, you can only use your passive losses to offset passive income. And that means you'll have to pay taxes on your regular income, no matter how much loss you can show on your property investments.

To add to the real estate investor blues, there's a problem with the inflation machine: the Federal Reserve turned it off for a while. Real estate appreciation, which relies heavily on inflation, just hasn't been the wild beast it was a few years ago. It was once true that even if you paid too much for a property today, you could always make a profit by holding onto it for a week. No longer; investors have to buy with care. In some parts of the country, for the first time in 20 years or more, prices are moving down rather than up. Keeping a house for 10 years and reaping the appreciation profits just isn't a workable strategy at this time.

About the only advantage to keeping a property nowadays is that rents continue to climb. Eventually the loan will be paid off, and buying a rental property today and keeping it for the rest of your life may be the smartest social security plan you can provide for yourself.

SO WHY FORECLOSURES?

First let's establish, that in a market with few tax advantages and slow growth, the real money is to be made by buying and selling quickly. And we've discussed that strategy. It means finding the best of all possible deals, snatching them up, and reselling them below market value—but making a few thousand dollars at the same time. Sure, it's challenging, but that's what this book is all about.

The problem: Find a piece of real estate, purchase it at about 60% of its market value, and resell it at about 80% of value, pocketing the other 20%.

It shouldn't be a real brainteaser to figure out that the second part—the selling—is going to be the easy half of the deal. The hard part is going to be finding a seller who will sell her $80,000 home for only $50,000. Would you?

The answer—foreclosures. Or, to be more accurate, homes *about to go into* foreclosure. To give you the gist of this book in a sentence: *Owners facing foreclosure would rather get a portion of their equity than none at all.*

You should, by now, have questions on the tip of your finger. You should be curious about foreclosures. You should be wondering just how common they are, and how you can find them and buy them and reap the tremendous profit we're promising. Well, you've come to the right book.

To really understand the foreclosure situation today, we have to look back a couple of years. Actually, we could go back to the Great Depression and follow the history of foreclosures to get a real feel for what's happening today. Did you know, for example, that there are more foreclosures today than ever before in the United States? We are standing knee deep in a flood of foreclosures, and before things get any better the flood will be up around our waists.

The accompanying graph should make the point. As you

can see, the number of foreclosures jumps right off the chart as we approach the present. And, at least for the next couple of years, there will continue to be more and more every day.

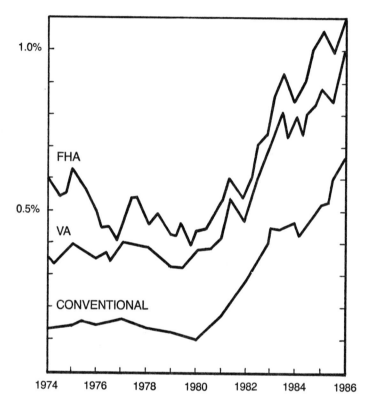

Percentage of Loans in Foreclosure
1974-1986
Source: Mortgage Bankers Assoc. of America

WHY SO MANY?

When the decade of the 1980s opened, lenders found themselves treading turbulent financial waters. Interest rates had skyrocketed, and they were paying out higher rates on savings accounts than they could collect on real estate loans. To counteract this disaster, they raised the rates on new loans, which, of course, raised the monthly payments so high that few new owners could afford to buy.

For the first time in history, bankers actually had to be creative! They came up with Adjustable Rate Mortgages (ARMs), Shared Equity Mortgages (SEMs), and—the real heart of the foreclosure problem, Graduated Payment Mortgages (GPMs). Before the dust had settled, there were dozens of half-breed mortgages created to lure new buyers without sacrificing profits, with such acronyms as FRM, RAM, SAM, PLAM, DIL, AML, VRM, RRM, and FLEX.

In every corner of the nation, homeowners who strapped themselves into a GPM did so knowing that they had agreed to pay a higher monthly payment every year for the first five years (in most cases). The same scene was played out again in kitchen after kitchen:

"But honey, that means in five years our house payment will be over $1500. We can't afford that!"

"We can't afford it now, maybe, but in five years we'll probably be making twice as much as we are now, and—"

"But you don't know that. What if we're not making any more? We'll lose the house!"

"C'mon. I'm making almost twice as much now as I was a year ago, and you are due for a raise next month. Besides, this is the only way we're ever going to get into a home of our own . . ."

That was five years ago.

Today, banks everywhere are forced to take back properties they don't want. Owners are forced to pack up and move back to the apartments. And for investors willing to spend the time educating themselves, the opportunities for profits are practically endless. Now is the time to be investing, and foreclosures are the place to invest. Today foreclosures are up 200% over 1981, and up 600% over 1978. The official forecast is for a constantly increasing number of foreclosures for at least another five years.

According to a spokesperson for the Department of Housing and Urban Development, many foreclosures take place between the second and fifth years of a mortgage. The loans that were made three years ago are now at an all-time high risk. And the high-interest GPMs were one of the hottest loan programs around about three years ago. Again according to HUD, the late 1980s and early 1990s will see even higher foreclosure rates than ever before in history. And there's nothing anyone can do about it now.

YOU CAN INVEST IN FORECLOSURES

Your next question was going to be, "If foreclosures are so great, why isn't everyone investing in them?" And the answer is simple—misinformation and misconception. The following are a few of the most common misconceptions we've heard:

"You need a lot of cash to buy foreclosure properties."

False. Once you know the rules of the game, all you need is knowledge. The money can always be found; if you don't have it, you can find someone who does.

In later chapters we will discuss sources of capital, from partners to bankers to sellers. And we'll show you, step by step, how we purchased a property facing foreclosure without any cash out of our pockets whatsoever.

"People who invest in foreclosures are vultures preying on the unfortunate."

False. People who invest in foreclosures aren't preying on anyone. If they buy the house before it goes to auction, they are saving the seller's credit rating; if they buy it at or after auction, they are saving the lender a horrible financial headache.

In Chapter 3, when you meet Gus and Doreen Johnson, you'll get a first-hand look at the difference between the vulture/shark/villain image (imposed on foreclosure specialists by ignorant critics) and reality.

"There are too many investors already; I couldn't compete with them for the same properties."
False. If the competition were that fierce, banks wouldn't have to be taking back thousands of homes every week. As the statistics already presented prove, you have no reason to fear a shortage of foreclosure properties—the supply far outstrips the demand by investors.

A surprisingly large number of foreclosure students are troubled by thoughts of competition. They envision hordes of investors swarming down on one property, robbing them of the opportunity to invest.

Fearing other investors is ridiculous. For one thing, many investors use the classified ads and Realtors to find property. They don't do much research. Second, with more and more properties going into foreclosure all the time, there isn't one investor in the world who can possibly follow up every lead. Third, most people who learn these techniques will either never put them to use or quit after they have bought one property and solved whatever problem pushed them into investing in the first place. Fourth, the other investors out there should be your friends; your first source of partners, leads, advice and money.

"You have to be a lawyer or trustee or some other expert to buy foreclosures safely and profitably."

False. You don't have to be an anything to buy foreclosure properties. You should, of course, be an expert, but that expertise can be learned. The misconception is in thinking that you can't become an expert. That expertise can be gained quite easily if you are willing to try.

Even if you never buy a single property at a foreclosure sale you can still make money by *buying from the owners before the sale,* and you obviously don't have to be an attorney to do that.

"If buying foreclosures is so great, every Realtor in the nation would be buying them."

Nothing could be further from the truth. Realtors, in general, don't even understand as much about the foreclosure process as you do at this point. Foreclosures are the skeletons in real estate's closet—nobody much likes to talk about them, much less study them. Some Realtors will buy distressed properties, if they fall into their laps, but they are not involved in actively pursuing leads, looking for good deals.

Many times a Realtor will be listing a property totally unaware that the owner is facing foreclosure. Owners are afraid to tell their listing agent that there is a foreclosure involved; they don't want to drive the price down.

We were amazed at the general level of ignorance on the subject exhibited by Realtors we talked to. And then we discovered why: They work in the retail market—in the department store of real estate. Buying foreclosures is like waiting around the back of the store for the damaged merchandise to be thrown out. By the time you have finished this book you will know more about foreclosures than the average Realtor anywhere in the nation.

There is no good reason for not investing in foreclosures, once you learn how to do it. You don't need a license, or a degree, or 10 years' experience to make money in real estate.

IF YOU MUST INVEST, MAKE IT PAY

Your choice of investments is nearly infinite, but one thing is clear: you must invest just to stay alive. Your investment can be 40 hours a week slinging burgers under shadow of the golden arches. You can strap yourself to a desk 60 hours a week and live the highly rewarding life of a migraine-and-heart-attack executive. You can scrimp and save every penny and hope that the interest on your HappySaver passbook account will ensure your financial independence.

Our argument is that if you have to invest, you might as well make it pay a high return. And foreclosures offer the highest return, with the least risk, of any investment we've found.

Foreclosure investing isn't the answer for everyone. It requires dedication, a willingness to work, and another dozen assorted characteristics that many people lack. Money won't fall from the sky just because you have decided to invest in foreclosure properties. However, if you're willing to sacrifice, to invest your time, energy, and a maybe a little money as well, this is one investment that can create a lifetime of financial security.

What sacrifices are you willing to make to reach your long-range financial goals? How many leisure hours are you willing to give up? If you can't promise yourself at least 10 hours a week for the next year, please give this book to a friend and save yourself the frustration.

Before you put the book down, however, take this thought to bed and sleep on it: If you do what you've always done, you'll go where you've always gone and you'll be what you've always been. If you're dissatisfied with your current situation, or if you want to enjoy a brighter financial future, read on.

CHAPTER TWO

The Foreclosure Process

You've already seen the rough shape of the beast we call "foreclosure." Now you're about to be introduced face to face. There are actually many sales of both real and personal property that fall under the general category of *forced sales*.

THE FORECLOSURE PROCESS

A true foreclosure occurs when a mortgage lender takes away the right of the borrower to redeem the debt. In many states there is no real "foreclosure." Rather, there is a "trustee's sale" or "sheriff's sale." However, you're probably more familiar with the term foreclosure, (which may bring to mind images of poor Pauline thrown out into the snow with her grandmother by the evil banker), we'll use that expression throughout this book.

For our purposes, a foreclosure is any forced sale of real property that can be purchased by an investor. As a legal definition it's admittedly wishy-washy, but, as you'll learn, you don't have to get hung up on legal definitions as long as you can accomplish your objective—making money. And we've found that once you cut through the legal definitions the whole subject is pretty easy to understand.

DEFINITIONS

This section is filled with terms that may be new to you. It is important that you commit these terms to memory, along with their definitions because if you are serious about investing you will be working with them extensively.

Two words that should already be a part of your vocabulary are *lien* and *encumbrance*. To dispel any chance that you don't fully understand them, here are their real estate definitions:

> *lien*. A hold or claim on property for the payment of a debt or obligation.
>
> *encumbrance*. A claim, lien or charge against real property that diminishes the value but does not prevent the transfer of fee title.

Throughout this chapter—and the remainder of the book—we'll use both terms, especially lien (because it's easier to spell), to mean any claim on real estate, from a mortgage to a mechanic's lien.

There are two basic instruments used for buying real estate: the *trust deed* and the *mortgage,* and which one is used varies from state to state. (You can call any title company, Realtor, or attorney in your area to find out which is used in your home state.)

The most common, and the one we'll use for examples in this book, is the trust deed, or *deed of trust.*

There are three parties involved in a sale by deed of trust: the *beneficiary*, the *trustee*, and the *trustor.*

The *beneficiary* is the lender—usually a bank or savings and loan. To commit the term to memory, remember that in the case of foreclosure it will be the lender who "benefits" from the sale. However, few institutional lenders consider foreclosing a real benefit.

The *trustor* is the borrower—the homeowner. We have no suggestions for remembering the term, unless you put yourself in the position of the borrower and then remember that you're the trustor. Use any method you can think of, but memorize the label and attach it to the right person. A foreclosure specialist like yourself needs a specialized vocabulary, and "trustor" is a basic part of the language.

The *trustee* is a third party (usually a lawyer, a title company, or a bank) hired by the lending institution to act on its behalf in the case of default. It is the trustee's job to bring about the foreclosure in the case of default; hence, the term "trustee's sale." Some lenders have in-house trustees whose job is to handle the foreclosure process, but most banks hire outside experts. In many states anyone who is proficient in the foreclosure process can be a trustee. In other states, such as Utah, there are restrictions on who can be a trustee.

A clever mnemonic device (at least we think it's clever, but then we made it up) for remembering who the trustee is: The lender (the beneficiary) depends on its "trusty trustee" to do the dirty work of foreclosing.

To better understand the process of the sale, start at the point where the borrower actually begins the whole process by purchasing real property.

At the time of the sale, two documents are executed: a *trust note* and a *deed of trust*. The trust note is signed by the borrower (the trustor) acknowledging the debt and includes a repayment schedule. The *deed of trust* is (in legalese):

> A deed that conveys real estate to a third person, to be held for the benefit of a beneficiary, with the power of sale upon default, and upon a trust to apply the net proceeds to paying the debt and to turn over the surplus

to the grantor (borrower).

If you aren't fluent in legalese, a rough translation is that the third party (the trustee) holds the title to the property until the debt is paid. If the borrower defaults, the trustee has the right and the obligation to sell the property. The trustee uses the proceeds of the sale to pay off the debt, and any money left over (equity) goes to the borrower.

The accompanying illustration of the first page of a trust deed, or deed of trust, merits some study so you can see the nature of such a document. To see what a complete, four-page trust deed looks like, complete with fine print, ask your local title officer for a blank copy of the one she uses.

Trust deeds are used by:

- □ FHA insured loans
- □ VA insured loans
- □ Farm Home Administration loans
- □ Conventional loans—commercial institutions
- □ Conventional loans—non-commercial institutions
- □ Conventional loans—individuals (seller carry-back loans)
- □ Small Business Administration loans

A *trustee's sale* (what we will be calling a foreclosure) occurs when the sale of real property has been secured by a trust deed. The trustee's sale is a *non-judicial* process to foreclose a lien created by the trust deed.

In states that do not use a deed of trust, such as Florida and Tennessee, a mortgage and promissory note are used. In these states the actual sale is called a foreclosure, rather than a trustee's sale, but the mechanics are largely the same. Since there is no trust deed, there can be no trustor or trustee. Instead there is a "mortgagor" (borrower) and a "mortgagee" (lender).

If the mortgage doesn't have a "power of sale" clause, the mortgagee must sell the property through a *judicial* proceed-

WHEN RECORDED. MAIL TO.

TRACY MORTGAGE COMPANY

465 East 200 South

Salt Lake City, Utah 84111

LOAN NO. 72039

SPACE ABOVE THIS LINE FOR RECORDER'S USE

STATE OF UTAH
FHA FORM NO. 2183-T
Rev. January 1977

TRUST DEED

With Assignment of Rents

This form is used in connection with deeds of trust insured under the one- to four-family provisions of the National Housing Act.

3822792

THIS TRUST DEED. made this ___22nd___ day of ___July___ . 19_83_.

BETWEEN___ DONALD CAL CAMPBELL and CINDY RAE CAMPBELL, his wife ___

_____. AS TRUSTOR.

whose address is___ 2602 South Melville Drive   Magna   Utah   84044
              (Street and number)   *(City)*   *(State)*

TRACY-COLLINS BANK AND TRUST COMPANY, a Utah Corporation ___. as TRUSTEE. and

TRACY MORTGAGE COMPANY, a Utah Corporation ___. as BENEFICIARY.

WITNESSETH: That Trustor CONVEYS and WARRANTS to TRUSTEE IN TRUST. WITH POWER OF SALE. the following described property. situated in ___Salt Lake___ County. State of Utah:

All of Lot 134, GREEN MEADOW ESTATES NO. 3, according to the official plat there of on file and of record in the Salt Lake County Recorder's Office.

TOGETHER WITH all buildings. fixtures and improvements thereon and all water rights. rights of way. easements. rents. issues. profits. income. tenements. hereditaments. privileges and appurtenances thereunto belonging. used or enjoyed with said property. or any part thereof. SUBJECT. HOWEVER. to the right. power and authority hereinafter given to and conferred upon Beneficiary to collect and apply such rents. issues. and profits. Without limiting the generality of the foregoing. the following described household appliances are deemed to be fixtures and a part of the realty. and are a portion of the security for the indebtedness herein mentioned:

FOR THE PURPOSE OF SECURING performance of each agreement of Trustor herein contained and the payment of the principal sum of ___FORTY FOUR THOUSAND FIFTY AND NO/100---Dollars (\$ 44,050.00). as evidenced by a promissory note. bearing even date herewith. for the payment of said principal sum. with interest thereon at the rate of ___TWELVE AND ONE-HALF___ per centum(12.500 %) per annum until paid: both principal sum and the interest thereon being payable in monthly installments at the times and in the amounts as set forth in said promissory note reference to which is here made. at the office of the Beneficiary in ___Salt Lake City, Utah___ ___ or at such other place as the holder may designate in writing. the final payment of principal and interest. if not sooner paid. shall be due and payable on the first day of ___AUGUST___ 2013

1. Privilege is reserved to pay the debt secured hereby in whole or in an amount equal to one or more principal payments next due on the note. on the first day of any month prior to maturity .provided written notice of intention so to do is given at least 30 days prior to prepayment.

27

ing. That is, the court must handle the sale. Another type of forced sale, the "sheriff's sale," is also a judicial sale, and follows the same rules. In the case of a judicial sale, the owner has a redemption period after the sale—as much as six months, depending on the state—during which he or she may make restitution and reclaim the property.

In the case of trust deeds (and trustees sales) and mortgages with the power of sale, the lender may sell the property without going through the court, a *non-judicial* sale, and there is no right of redemption.

For simplicity's sake, as well as our peace of mind, we steer clear of judicial sales. Who wants to buy a property and then wait six months while the owner decides whether or not to redeem it?

The only advantage to lenders in going through the court system is that they may obtain a *deficiency judgment* in a judicial proceeding of foreclosure. In a non-judicial sale, the beneficiary cannot get a deficiency judgment. We'll talk more about these judgments later. We don't want to overload your vocabulary circuits all at once.

It's important, as we've mentioned already, to find out what laws govern the rules of foreclosure in your own state. Before you begin investing it wouldn't hurt to spend a Saturday afternoon at the local law library, reading your state's statutes that deal with foreclosures and trustee's sales. Most law libraries come equipped with at least one excellent librarian who will help you find what you're looking for.

Let's review. You should be familiar with each of the following terms:

□ Trust Deed	□ Mortgagee
□ Trust Note	□ Promissory Note
□ Trustor	□ Judicial Sale
□ Trustee	□ Non-judicial Sale

- Beneficiary
- Mortgage
- Mortgagor

- Foreclosure
- Trustee's Sale
- Redemption Period

If any one of the above terms throws you, go back and reread this section, or check the glossary, before going on. It's like any language class: If you miss the basic vocabulary, you'll be lost forever.

THE TRUSTEE'S SALE (FORECLOSURE)

Trust deeds have been increasing in popularity over mortgage notes, and one day may be the only method of selling real estate. Therefore, trustee's sales will continue to be the mainstay of the foreclosure world, and you should acquaint yourself thoroughly with the process.

A foreclosure begins, of course, with a default—a "failure of a party to fulfill a contractual obligation or to perform some duty." In the case of a trust deed, the trustor fails to make one or more payments on his loan.

The trust note will usually call for a monthly payment. However, it may demand a payment only quarterly, semi-annually, annually, or any combination of the above. As a rule, in fairness to the borrower, a foreclosure cannot take place until at least two *monthly* payments have been missed. For all other repayment schedules, a foreclosure may begin after only one missed payment. Find out what the laws are in your own state.

There are five steps in a foreclosure:
1) Default and collection attempt.
2) Notice of default/Cancellation of notice of default.
3) Notice of sale/Cancellation of notice of sale.
4) Day of sale.
5) After the sale.

Money can be made by an investor before, during and after the sale, *if* the entire process is thoroughly understood. We'll study each phase of a foreclosure in depth:

Default and Collection Attempt

A lending institution will generally go out of its way to collect payments in arrears before resorting to foreclosure. When the first payment is missed, a nicely worded letter is sent. Something along the lines of: "Dear Homeowner, you are behind on your payment. We realize this may be a simple oversight on your part. We would appreciate your prompt payment."

After the second month, another letter, couched in not-so-nice terms is sent, reminding the owner that he or she may be facing foreclosure and again asking for immediate payment. This letter will be followed by another, which will be followed by phone calls. At this point, both the bank and the owner are getting quite concerned about the missing payments. Some owners simply pack up and move, deserting the property.

When, after several attempts, it becomes apparent that foreclosure is necessary, the beneficiary will turn the matter over to the trustee by delivering a copy of the original note and deed of trust and demanding that foreclosure be started.

Notice of Default (NOD)

The trustee appointed by the beneficiary will create and record (in the county courthouse) a "notice of default" (NOD). The purpose of the notice is to let interested parties know that the loan is delinquent to the point of foreclosure, and action has begun to sell the property under the provisions of the trust deed according to the laws of the state.

Within 10 days of recording, a copy of the notice will be

sent by registered mail to the address shown on the trust deed. Additionally, a copy of the notice must be mailed to each trustor at his last known address if different than the address specified in the deed of trust.

The trustee has a legal obligation to get word to the trustors that they are in default. In cases where the trustors have not requested to be notified in the deed of trust, or if the address in the deed is not sufficient for the trustee to make contact, then the trustee will advertise the notice in a newspaper published in the county where the property is situated. The notice will be published once a week for four weeks, giving the trustors enough time to spot it—provided they read the classified ads.

The alternative to printing a copy of the notice in the newspaper is personal service—tracking down the trustors and placing a copy in their hot little hands. Naturally, trustees prefer to publish.

The trustee may also be required to mail the same notice to all junior lien claimants, but they don't have to be notified until a full month after the recording.

Sorry to interrupt the flow, but we must sidestep here for a moment and address the subject of *junior* and *senior liens*. The subject has a great impact on the entire foreclosure process and, therfore, on your investing strategies.

Whenever there is a lien against a piece of real estate—that is, any debt or obligation secured by the property—it must be recorded. Recording takes place when someone makes a public record of the debt in the county courthouse. By making the lien a matter of public record, the lender is putting the public on notice that he or she has the right to make a claim against the property when and if it becomes necessary.

It's like "first dibs," when you're a kid and you want to secure your legal right to the glow-in-the-dark Cap'n in the next box of Cap'n Crunch. You shout, "I get first dibs on the Cap'n!" thereby publicly staking your claim. You've recorded your lien.

Junior and senior liens are easily explained along the same lines. If your sister yells first, her lien is senior to yours. If your brother yells after you, his lien is junior to yours and to your sister's.

Likewise, when a second beneficiary records a lien after the first, it is called a "junior lien," at least with respect to the first lien. The newly recorded lien will, of course, be senior to any liens recorded after that point.

Getting back to the main subject, most states require that the foreclosing beneficiary give notice to all junior lien holders. In some states (and it changes often, so check with a local attorney) the beneficiary doesn't have to give notice unless the junior claimants have filed a *request for notice of default*. (As a side note, if you ever sell property and carry a note of your own, in a subordinate position to another lien, you should always file such a request.)

An extremely important point arises here that we'll discuss in detail shortly: In a foreclosure, all liens junior to the one being foreclosed are absolved at the time of the sale, unless someone bids enough at auction to cover them. Senior liens remain "attached" to the property, by definition. Remember the Cap'n? Senior lien holders have first dibs, and their claims against the property are unaffected by the sale.

Most states do not require a specific form for a notice of default, but a notice should contain all of the following and look like the accompanying (blank) NOD form:

□ The borrower's name (trustor).*
□ The lender's name (beneficiary).*
□ Repayment schedule.
□ Legal description.*

- Dollar amount of each payment.
- Number of payments delinquent.
- Original loan amount.
- Original loan date.
- Date the loan was recorded.*

*Usually required by law.

Notice of Default Form

NOTICE IS HEREBY GIVEN:
That ABC Title Company is Trustee under a Deed of Trust dated
_____, 19____, executed by _____,
and _____, his wife, as Trustors, to secure a certain
obligation in favor of _____, as Beneficiary, recorded
_____ 19 _____, as Entry No. _____ in Book _____ at
Page _____ of the official records in the office of the County Recorder of
_____ County, State of Utah, describing the land therein as:

Said obligation includes a note for the original principal sum of
$_____

The Beneficial interest under such Deed and the obligation secured
thereby are now owned by _____.

A breach of and default in the obligation for which said Deed is secured
has occurred in that payment has not been made of the following:

TOTAL AMOUNT DUE: $_____
By reason of such default, ABC Title Company, as Trustee, and
_____, as Beneficiary, under said Deed of
Trust, do hereby declare all sums secured thereby immediately due and
payable and have elected and do hereby elect to cause the trust property
to be sold to satisfy the obligations secured thereby.

DATED this _____ day of _____, 19____.

_____
ABC Title Company, Trustee
100 E. Center Street
Salt Lake City, Utah 84111

STATE OF UTAH

County of Salt Lake
On this _____ day of _____, 19____,
personally appeared before me _____, Trustee,
the signer of the within instrument, who duly acknowledged to me that he
executed the same.

_____
NOTARY PUBLIC
Residing at Salt Lake City, Utah

My commission expires:

_____

The following sample notice of default (NOD) is an actual copy (with a few details changed to protect the privacy of those involved) of an NOD that was published in a newspaper not long ago.

Published Notice of Default

NOTICE IS HEREBY GIVEN: That Zion Title, Inc. is the Successor Trustee under a Trust Deed dated June 6, 1975, executed by John Doe and Betty Doe, his wife, as trustors, to secure certain obligations in favor of XYZ Savings and Loan Company, as Beneficiary, which Trust Deed was recorded on June 7, 1975, as Entry No. 23454 in Book 4523 at Page 234 of the official records in the Office of the County Recorder of Salt Lake County, Utah, which covers the following trust property:

> Lot 2 Happy Valley Subdivision No. 1 as recorded in the office of the Salt Lake County Recorder.

That a breach of obligations for which the trust property was conveyed as security has occurred, in that the monthly payments have not been made as agreed.

That, by reason of such breach, XYZ Savings and Loan Company, a Beneficiary, and Zion Title, Inc., as Successor Trustee, under said Trust Deed, do hereby declare all sums secured thereby immediately due and payable, and do hereby elect to sell or cause the trust property to be sold to satisfy these obligations.

DATED this 2nd day of June, 1985
Zion Title, Inc., Successor Trustee

What were you looking for in all that legalese? The following:

- Name of the borrower.
- Date the loan was recorded.
- Courthouse entry number, the book and the page.
- Name of the trustee or the successor trustee.
- Name of the beneficiary.
- Legal description of the property.

◻ Original loan amount.

◻ Why the loan violates the terms of the deed: missing payments, advances to a superior lien claimant, non-payment of property taxes, transfer of property ownership without the lender's consent, etc.

Some NODs will give useful additional information, such as:

1) The dollar amount of the monthly payments.

2) The street address.

3) The trustee's phone number and/or address.

4) A statement informing the owner that there is a 90-day reinstatement period.

The sample NODs on the following pages are packed with useful information. Read them carefully and see if you can decipher them and extract the useful information.

The trustee may or may not be required, depending on the state and the circumstances, to send a second notice 30 days after recording the notice. This is likely to be the case only when the real property is a single family, owner-occupied home.

The second notice, which is again mailed to the last known address of the trustor, will say something like this:

YOU ARE IN DEFAULT UNDER A

_____
(Deed of Trust or Mortgage)

DATED _____. UNLESS YOU TAKE ACTION TO PROTECT YOUR HOME, IT MAY BE SOLD AT A PUBLIC SALE. IF YOU NEED AN EXPLANATION OF THE NATURE OF THE PROCEEDING AGAINST YOU, YOU SHOULD CONTACT A LAWYER.

**Notice of Default
(Example 1)**

NOTICE IS HEREBY GIVEN: That Continental Savings is the Successor Trustee under a Trust Deed dated December 14, 1982, executed by John Doe Construction Company, through John Doe, President, as Trustors, to secure certain obligations in favor of Happy Valley Easy Loan Company, as Beneficiary, which Trust Deed was recorded on December 15, 1982, as Entry No. 12234, in Book 1234 at Page 345 of the official records in the Office of the County Recorder of Salt Lake County, Utah, which covers the following described trust property:

Lot 1 Heavenly Valley Subdivision No. 1 as recorded in the office of the Salt Lake County Recorder.

That the breach of obligations for which the trust property was conveyed as security has occurred, in that monthly payments have not been made of:

1) Principal and interest in the monthly amount of $227.03.
2) The additional sum of $1,757.32, which sum was advanced by the Beneficiary to cure default on the subject property at XYZ Loan Company.

That, by reason of such breaches, Happy Valley Easy Loan Company, Beneficiary, and Continental Savings, as Successor Trustee, under said Trust Deed, do hereby declare all sums secured thereby immediately due and payable, and do hereby elect to sell or cause the trust property to be sold to satisfy these obligations.

DATED This 23rd day of February, 1985
Continental Savings
Successor Trustee

Cancellation of Notice of Default

The recording of a notice of default does not mean the borrower has reached the point of no return. There is a reinstatement period following the recording of the NOD that varies from state to state. The most common period is 90 days, but it can be as short as 30 days. The NOD may be cancelled any time within the reinstatement period. To do so, the borrower—subsequent owner, or junior lien holder—must bring the loan current, including all late charges, accrued interest and trustee's fees—which are generally set by state statute. After the reinstatement period, the lender *may* have the option of accepting or rejecting an attempt to cure the default.

As a note of interest and a point of legality, you should know that the NOD must be recorded with the county recorder. If it is not recorded, or if there is an error in the legal

Notice of Default
(Example 2)

NOTICE IS HEREBY GIVEN: That Continental Savings is the Successor Trustee under a Trust Deed dated january 5, 1984, executed by John Doe and Betty Doe, his wife, as Trustors, to secure certain obligations in favor of XYZ Savings and Loan Company, as Beneficiary, which Trust Deed was recorded on January 5, 1984, as Entry No. 23454 in Book 2143 at Page 345 of the official records in the Office of the County Recorder of Salt Lake County, Utah, which covers the following described trust property:

Lot 3 Heavenly Valley Subdivision No. 1 as recorded in the office of the Salt Lake County Recorder.

That the breach of obligations for which the trust property was conveyed as security has occurred, in that the monthly payments have not been made since March 5, 1984.
1) Monthly payments of $435.16
2) Reserve for taxes and insurance of $435.16
3) Trustee's fees and costs.

That, by reason of such breach, XYZ Savings and Loan Company, as Beneficiary, and Continental Savings, as Successor Trustee, under said Trust Deed, do hereby declare all sums secured thereby immediately due and payable, and do hereby elect to sell the trust property to satisfy these obligations, all as provided for by Title 57, Chapter 1, Utah Code Annotated (1983), as amended and supplemented.
DATED this 23rd day of February, 1985
Continental Savings
Successor Trustee

description of the property, the trustee's sale may be invalid.

If the trustor doesn't bring the loan current, it may be reinstated by a junior lien claimant, who can then foreclose on his own mortgage. The rule governing such an action is called *endangered collateral.* By defaulting on the first mortgage, the trustor has endangered the interest of all the latter mortgage holders. As a result, each of them has the right to bring the first mortgage current within the reinstatement period and then start a foreclosure proceeding of their own.

When a junior lien claimant brings a defaulted loan current, thereby cancelling the NOD, the original foreclosure is immediately cancelled. Therefore, if the junior claimant exercises his right to foreclose, he must institute a new foreclosure action, including a new notice of default.

To get a better picture of the problem faced by a junior lien claimant, study the following example:

A piece of property has four liens against it—two and three are very common today.

1st Lien: Savings & Loan	$ 50,000
2nd Lien: Thrift & Loan	$ 20,000
3rd Lien: Credit Union	$ 10,000
4th Lien: Prior Owner	$ 5,000
Equity	$ 40,000
Market Value	$125,000

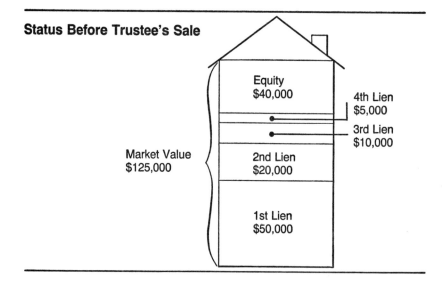

Status Before Trustee's Sale

Equity $40,000

4th Lien $5,000

3rd Lien $10,000

Market Value $125,000

2nd Lien $20,000

1st Lien $50,000

When the trustor defaults on the first mortgage, and the Savings & Loan forecloses, the lowest bid will be for $50,000—to cure the defaulted debt. If nobody else bids, the Savings & Loan will bid at least that amount to protect its interest. If the property is sold for $50,000, all junior liens will be wiped out—literally cease to exist. That puts Thrift & Loan, the Credit Union, and the prior owner in a tough spot: If, for example, the Credit Union wants to protect its interest it must go to the sale and bid at least $50,001 to get the property. And if the Thrift & Loan shows up at the sale, ready to protect its lien, the Credit Union will have to bid $70,001 to cover the first two liens. If the prior owner, in fourth position, wants to salvage his $5,000 interest, he may have to bid—and pay in cash—$80,001. That's not a bad price for a home with a $125,000 market value, but the prior owner may not be able to get $80,001 in cash.

With the right to reinstate a superior claim prior to sale, the junior claimant (who wisely filed a request for notice of default) can do so and pick up a property at a substantial discount.

BORROWER'S OPTIONS

The trustor has five options when he receives his NOD:

□ He may cancel it by bringing the loan current, as already discussed.

□ He may allow the sale to take place, deserting the premises now or waiting for the sheriff to bring a moving van to the house in a gesture of community thoughtfulness.

□ He may trade the property for another, leaving the default for the new owner.

□ He may sell the property.

□ He may try to give the property to the lender.

We don't need to dwell further on the first two options, so we'll discuss the other three.

Trading the Property

When a trustor trades his property for another, the default of the trust deed stays with the property. Therefore, the new owner takes title subject to all existing liens against the property. It is the new owner's responsibility to cure the NOD within the reinstatement period.

If the new owner in such a case is unaware of the NOD, it is only because he or she failed to have a title search done. A search would have revealed the clouded title, and the new owner could have insisted that the seller cure the default, or would have at least been prepared for the problem.

Selling the Property Before the Trustee's Sale
Many owners, after three months of missed payments, will realize the futility of fighting foreclosure, and will try to sell their home. Again, the new owner takes title subject to all existing liens, and faces the same situation as the new owner who traded property. But many sellers in default are happy to walk away from most or all of their equity if someone offers to cure a problem that's been giving them ulcers for three months. (That's what the next two chapters are all about.)

In a recent case, an owner ran the following ad:

> *Must sell this week. Appraised $50,000,*
> *Will sell for only $42,000—$4,000 down.*
> *Call 555-2343*

He had listed his home for three months with an incompetent real estate agent, who had assured him the home would sell easily for $52,000. During the entire three-month listing period, the owner hadn't made a payment; he was going to have the buyer make the missed payments. When, at the end of three months, the home hadn't sold, he was desperate. A notice of default had been filed by the bank. He couldn't cure the default, and foreclosure was imminent. With one phone call, Jim, a foreclosure investor, found out the following:

There was only one lien against the property, the original loan, for $38,000. The home's actual market value was approximately $49,000, leaving $11,000 equity. The monthly payment was $355, including principal, interest, taxes and insurance. The bank needed only $1,200 to cure the default.

Jim offered (and his offer was accepted) $500 for the owner's equity, with the buyer to assume the existing loan, cure the default, and pay all closing costs. For less than $2,000 cash, the investor purchased the home for approximately $40,000, picking up $9,000 instant equity. The entire process took two weeks—part time.

Giving the Property to the Lender—"Deed in lieu of"

The property owner may give the property to the lender "in consideration of the trust note being paid in full and the seller having no liability for said trust note and deed." If the lender accepts the property, the default is cured and that's the end of the problem. However, for conveyance to be valid, it must be accepted by the lender. Naturally, if the value of the property is greater than the amount of the debt, the lender will be inclined to accept it.

According to a recent article in *NEWSWEEK* magazine, it has become a common tactic for owners in default to simply mail the front door key to the lender, a quick and almost painless way of saying, "We give up."

If the notice of default is cancelled by any of the methods discussed, the trustee will file a "Cancellation of Notice of Default." This document serves as public notice that the default has been cured in one way or another.

NOTICE OF SALE (NOS)

After the reinstatement period has expired, the trustee will contact the beneficiary to make sure there has been no cancellation. If the default has continued, the trustee will proceed with a Notice of Sale.

The notice of sale is sent, via registered mail, to the same

Cancellation of Notice of Default

The undersigned hereby cancels the Notice of Default filed for record on _____, and recorded as Entry No. _____ in the records of the County Recorder of Salt Lake County, State of Utah which Notice of Default refers to the Trust Deed executed by _____, and his wife _____, as Trustor, in which Happy Valley Easy Loan Company of Utah was named as beneficiary, which was filed for record on _____, and recorded in Book _____, at Page _____, in the records of the County Recorder of Salt Lake County, State of Utah, covering the following described real property situated in Salt Lake County, State of Utah to wit:

_____

STATE OF UTAH	ABC Title Company, Trustee 100 E. Center Street Salt Lake City, Utah 84111

County of Salt Lake

On this _____ day of _____ 19____, personally appeared before me _____, Trustee, the signer of the within instrument, who duly acknowledged to me that he executed the same.

_____

NOTARY PUBLIC
Residing at Salt Lake City, Utah

My commission expires: _____

---

people as the NOD: the beneficiary, the trustor(s), the junior lienholders, and anyone who has filed a request for notice. It must contain all of the following information:

1) Date of Sale

The sale will be scheduled about 30 days after the notice of sale is initiated, but there are no absolutes; it is up to the trustee and the beneficiary to set the actual date and time. As a general rule, the sale will take place four to six weeks after the first publication of the notice of sale.

The sale can, by law, take place on any day of the week; however, as a common practice most foreclosure sales will not occur on a Saturday or Sunday or holiday.

2) Place of Sale

The place of sale must be in the county where the property is situated. The street address, or other common designation, must be specified in the Notice of Sale. If the place of sale has more than one entrance, the particular entrance at which the sale will be made must be specified.

3) *Time of Sale*

A time is specified in the notice, and it will usually be between 9:00 a.m. and 5:00 p.m. There have been stories told of unscrupulous trustees who, in collusion with equally unscrupulous beneficiaries, set the time, date, and location so that no one will show up to make a bid. Christmas Eve, at midnight, under an abandoned bridge might discourage a few would-be buyers. Fortunately, the vast majority of trustees are completely honest.

4) *Description*

The location of the property must be spelled out accurately and completely. The street address or other common designation will always be included, and possibly a complete legal description as it appears in the county register.

5) *Trustee's Name*

The trustee who prepares the notice and who will be conducting the sale must identify itself.

Publication and Posting

The NOS must be recorded at least 14 days prior to the day of sale. Furthermore, the sale *must* be advertised by publishing a NOS in a publication of general circulation within the county in which the property is located. The courts will determine which publications may be used, and it will vary from one jurisdiction to the next. In smaller areas, from rural to suburban, notices of sale will usually be published in local newspapers, just before the classified ads. In larger metropolitan areas they will often appear in legal journals and notices. To find out where they are published in your area, contact the State Newspaper Association nearest you (see list on page 206) or call your real estate attorney, the Bar Association in your state, or a local law school library.

The trustee must publish the notice of sale at least once a week for three weeks prior to the sale. For most investors, it is this public notice that gets the ball rolling.

In addition to publication, the NOS must be posted in two more places: First, in one public place in the city where the property is to be sold; and, second, in some conspicuous place on the property itself. In the case of a single family home the notice will usually be posted on the front door.

On the following page are two examples of notices of sale. By studying them you can learn to quickly read between the lines of a NOS and make sense of what might at first appear to be confusing legal jargon.

Cancellation of the Notice of Sale

After the reinstatement period expires, following the recording of the NOD, the lender may (depending upon applicable state laws) call the entire loan balance due and payable. This option will not be available to lenders in some states, another point on which you should familiarize yourself with your state's laws.

At this point it is up to the lender whether or not the default may be cured by simply making up the back payments and paying any legal fees incurred and interest accrued. This is, for most owners, the point of no return, and the expiration date of the NOD period is called the cure date.

If the notice of sale is not cancelled, the property will go to auction.

Notice of Trustee's Sale
(Example 1)

The following described property will be sold at public auction to the highest bidder on the 15th day of June, 1985, at 9:00 a.m., at the South ground level entrance of the Courts Building at Salt Lake City, by ABC Title Company, Trustee and Happy Valley Easy Loan Company of Utah, as Beneficiary, under the Deed of Trust made by John Doe and Betty Doe, his wife, as Trustors, recorded June 29, 1977, as Entry No. 12345 in Book 234 at page 12 of the official records of Salt Lake County, Utah given to secure an indebtedness in favor of said Beneficiary by reason of certain obligations secured thereby.

Notice of Default was recorded February 12, 1985, as Entry No. 12344 in Book 3454 at page 34 of said official records.

Trustee will sell at public auction to the highest bidder in cash, payable in lawful money of the United States at the time of sale, without warranty as to title, possession or encumbrances, the following described property at 2345 Happy Lane, Heaven:

All of lot 1, Heavenly Valley No. 1, according to the official plat thereof, on file and of record in the office of Salt Lake County Recorder.

for the purpose of paying obligations secured by said Deed of Trust including fees, charges and expenses of Trustee, advances, in any, under the terms of said Deed of trust, interest thereon and the unpaid principal of the note secured by said Deed of Trust with interest thereon as in said note and by law provided.

DATED this 15th day of May, 1985.
ABC Title Company
100 E. Center Street
Salt Lake City, Utah 84111

Notice of Trustee's Sale
(Example 2)

The following described property will be sold at public auction to the highest bidder at the North Front Doors of the County Court House in Salt Lake City, County of Salt Lake, State of Utah, on October 12, 1984, at 11:30 a.m. on said day.

Lot 1 Heavenly Valley No. 1, according to the plat thereof, as recorded in the Office of the County Recorder of said County.

Purchase price payable in lawful money of the United States.
DATED this 3rd day of September, 1984.
ABC Title Company, Trustee
100 E. Center Street
Salt Lake City, Utah 84111

FORECLOSURE CALENDAR

A typical foreclosure proceeding might look like this:

January 15	Trustor misses first payment; beneficiary sends nice letter, asking politely for the money.
February 15	Trustor misses second payment; beneficiary sends second letter, asking again for payment and notifying the trustor that he or she should contact the bank if there's a problem.
March 15	Trustor misses third payment; beneficiary sends third letter, threatening foreclosure. Beneficiary also contacts trustee to begin proceedings.
March 20	Trustee prepares a Notice of Default and records it with the county recorder. The three-month NOD clock begins ticking.
March 30	Trustee sends a copy of the NOD to the trustor via registered mail. If trustor cannot be contacted, the NOD will be published in a newspaper.
April 15	Trustor misses fourth payment; in many cases the property has been abandoned at this point.
April 20	If the default has not been cured, the trustee will send copies of the NOD to all junior lienholders and other parties who have filed a request for notice of default.
May 15	Trustor misses fifth payment; with five months in back payments, plus legal fees,

most trustors have lost any chance of recovering.

June 15 Trustor misses sixth payment; reinstatement period is almost over, and trustor is either "waiting it out," holding onto his or her castle until the last minute, or has abandoned the property.

June 20 Last day of three-month reinstatement period. For most trustors, the absolute last chance to cure the default on their own, although they may sell the property with the beneficiary's approval, which is rarely withheld.

June 27 First publication and posting of the Notice of Sale; copies are mailed to the trustors, the beneficiary, the junior lienholders, and other interested parties who have filed a request for notice.

July 4 The Fourth of July; parades, fireworks. Second publication of notice of sale.

July 14 Third publication.

August 2 Sale date.

DAY OF THE SALE

On the day of the sale, the trustee acts as the auctioneer. A representative from the trutee's office will conduct the sale in a public place, as advertised in the NOS, and will open the auction by reading the notice of sale, stating the terms of payment, and asking for an opening bid. If the trustee is authorized by the beneficiary to bid on its behalf, he or she will do so, opening the bidding with the amount necessary to pay the balance on the loan, including attorneys' fees, trustee's fees, and accrued interest.

In other words, the opening bid will automatically cover all debts thus far incurred.

Anyone may bid at the auction, including the original borrower, the new owner, the junior lien holders, or Joe from Joe's Bar and Grill down the street.

If there has been no postponement, the sale will take place at the exact time and place mentioned in the NOS. The auctioneer will read the entire notice of sale aloud and announce that the bid price must be paid in cash, lawful money of the United States, a cashier's check payable to the trustee and drawn on a state or national bank. If the beneficiary is the purchaser, the balance due on the trust deed may be offset against the bid price. In other words, the beneficiary doesn't have to make a cash bid to cover its own loan. However, a junior lienholder may not offset his lien against his bid price.

After reading the NOS, the auctioneer will make a formalized statement opening the auction and disclaiming all warranties regarding the condition of the property:

> *Now, therefore, I, on behalf of Trustee Guaranty, Incorporated, by virtue of the authority vested in it as trustee under deed of trust, offer at public auction the property described therein. Said sale is made without covenant or warranty either express or implied as to title, possession, or encumbrances.*
>
> *I do offer said property for any sum not less than the sum sufficient to pay the said total amount secured by deed of trust.*

The trustee will generally have a paid witness, who will begin the bidding by stating the beneficiary's bid:

On behalf of the beneficiary, I bid the sum of $_____.

After each bid, the trustee must state the amount of the bid and call for further bids. The auctioneer will then state, upon receiving the last bid, "Going once, going twice, last and final call. Going three times. Sold to _____ for $____."

Trustee's Deed

At most auctions, the winning bidder must pay the entire price in cash at the time of sale, or within a few hours.

At the conclusion of the sale the trustee will prepare a "trustee's deed" for the purchase, and ownership will pass from the trustor to the winner of the auction.

Under the provisions of the trustee's deed, the purchaser takes title to the property subject to all senior liens. This includes any liens recorded before the lien being foreclosed, and, in rare cases, liens that were recorded later but were actually in effect before the date of recordation. We'll get to this confusing subject in a minute).

The deed can only be in the name of the winning bidder; for example, if John Doe bids in his own name, he cannot later demand that the trustee deed be executed in favor of John Doe and Associates or JD Enterprises.

Disbursement

The trustee will pay the sale proceeds to the beneficiary with an accounting showing the deduction of trustee's fees. If the property sells for more than the amount demanded by the beneficiary, the surplus is turned over—through an *interpleader action*—to a court for disbursement. It is not the trustee's responsibility to determine how the excess money is to be divided.

The court will disburse all surplus money to the junior lien-holders in order of seniority. If there is anything left over, it will go to the trustor, but there is rarely anything left over.

Junior Liens and Senior Liens

As we have already mentioned, all liens junior to the one being foreclosed are extinguished at the time of sale. However, there will be exceptions. Federal tax debts are considered effective when they are incurred, regardless of when they are recorded. Some mechanic's liens (a debt owed to a contractor for work done on the property) are effective as of the date the work was done, whether or not they were recorded then.

Generally, all you'll need to concern yourself with in foreclosures is determining which liens are junior to the foreclosed lien, and which are senior.

Junior liens include all abstracts of judgment, leases, state tax liens that have the effect of a judgment; trust deeds, mortgages that are dated and recorded after the foreclosed deed of trust; and encumbrances that have been subordinated to the foreclosed trust deed. ("Subordination" occurs when a lien is recorded before another, but the holder of the note agrees to take a junior position to the second lien.)

Senior liens include all liens recorded before the foreclosed trust deed. They remain attached to the property after the sale, and the new owner is liable for them. Such liens may include:

□ Trust note and deed.   □ Judgments.
□ Mortgages.   □ Real estate contracts.
□ Property taxes.   □ Options.
□ Mechanic liens.   □ Some utility charges.

An explanation may be in order for some of the liens mentioned. You should already be familiar with the options.

If not, pick up a real estate primer and refresh your memory, or ask a Realtor for help.

A *mechanic lien* has already been briefly defined. If the owner of property has had any work done within the last 100 days, and if the labor or materials have not been paid for, the mechanic can record a lien against the property. That lien can be foreclosed on, and the mechanic can sell the property at auction to recover his or her damages.

A *judgment* is a court-appointed lien that occurs as the result of a civil suit. If the homeowner fails to pay Grocer Brown for his vegetables, Grocer Brown can sue and have a judgment placed on the home. Then, through a sheriff's sale, Grocer Brown can sell the home to recover his debt.

You know what *utility charges* are. What you may not know, however, is that the utility company may refuse to reconnect service if there is an unpaid balance. That means that if you buy a house for which the previous owner had discontinued paying the electricity bill, you might be faced with a warm refrigerator and a cold stove. If you took your case to court you would win, no doubt, but that would involve an expenditure of time and money that nobody can afford. A much better idea is to find out in advance of the sale if there are any delinquent utility bills.

You may still be feeling some confusion when you read about some liens getting wiped out and others surviving. We'll use illustrations to make the whole picture a little clearer.

Example
There are five liens against a property, and the owner only defaults on the third lien. If the trustee of that lien forecloses for only the amount of that debt, the new owner must assume liability for the first and second liens, which survive intact.

The fourth and fifth liens—the junior liens, in this case—are wiped out; they no longer exist.

Which liens are paid for, which are eliminated, and which remain depends upon who is foreclosing and how much is bid. Here's a test question:

A property has six liens against it. The second mortgage, for $40,000, held by ABC Mortgage Company, is in default, and the trustee for that mortgage has brought about the foreclosure sale. The fourth lien holder, a credit union, has a lien of $12,000, which it wants to protect. If nobody else shows up at auction (besides ABC Mortgage and the credit union), how much must the credit union bid, which loans are paid in full at the time of sale, and what happens to the remaining liens? (Don't continue reading until you have at least attempted to work out the problem.)

Answer: The credit union must make a cash bid high enough to satisfy ABC Mortgage's debt—in this case $40,001, plus any money needed to cover legal costs and accrued interest. The first mortgage survives intact; if it is assumable, the credit union will assume that loan; if it isn't, it will probably be due in full immediately. The third through the sixth mortgages are erased, including the credit union's; however, since the credit union bought the house at auction, its lien is well covered by the equity in the property. (This case would be very unlikely in actuality; the third mortgage holder would have been notified and would certainly have showed up to protect its interest.)

It is apparent that before an investor shows up at auction, he or she should already be familiar with all existing liens and, if possible, know who will and who will not show up at the auction. The existing liens and encumbrances will be revealed in a title search, and paying for title insurance gives the new owner the added assurance that if any prior liens aren't discovered at the time of the search, the title company will pay for the mistake.

If you are still confused, study the following diagrams. They detail several possible auction situations relating to a piece of property with a number of liens against it.

Status Before the Sale
(Example 1)

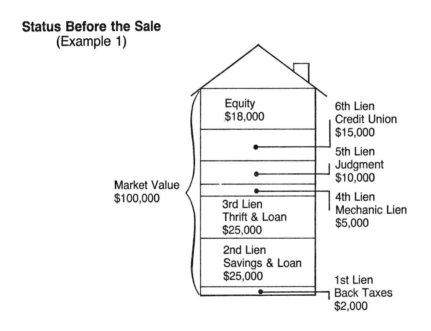

Status After the Sale
(Example 2)

In this example, the trustee's sale was conducted by the owner of the 5th lien, a Credit Union. The highest bidder (possibly the Credit Union itself) bid enough to pay the debt, taking ownership and assuming responsibility for the remaining liens and encumbrances. The liens total $67,000, leaving the new owner with $33,000 equity.

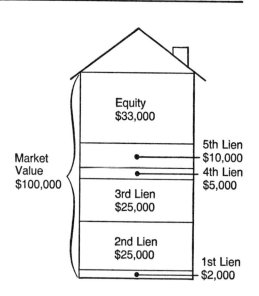

Status After the Sale
(Example 3)

In this case, the owners of the 2nd lien, a Thrift & Loan, foreclosed on its $25,000 debt. The highest bidder assumed the first and second liens, for a total of $27,000 debt, and acquired a $73,000 equity. It isn't apparent from the diagram whether the fourth, fifth and sixth liens were paid or dissolved. They may have all showed up for the sale, in which case the sixth lien holder would have had to bid enough to cover the fifth, fourth and third liens.

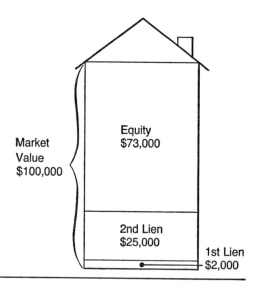

Let's back up and review. You should understand the entire foreclosure process, from the moment of default until the day of sale. You've learned a whole new vocabulary, and you're well versed in the process of who gets what, what gets wiped out, and which liens stay with the property after the sale . . . right? If there's any confusion, reread this chapter before proceeding. If you're stuck after two readings, go ahead and finish the book and then come back.

If you're reading this for the third time and you're still confused, contact a local expert. Ask your lender who they use as a trustee, and then, very politely, ask that trustee for a few minutes. If you're still lost, write to us:

FORTUNE BUSINESSES
PO Box 574
Orem, Utah 84057

If you're sure you understand how the game is played, let's move ahead and make you a player. In the next chapter you'll meet the losing team: the foreclosure victims. Theirs is not a pretty story, but, thanks to foreclosure specialists, it doesn't have to be a tragedy.

CHAPTER THREE

Finding The Great Deals

There is a story, said to have originated with Mark Twain, about a frog who fell into a wagon wheel rut and couldn't get out. It was too deep, and try as he might he couldn't reach the top. His friends came by and offered to help, but their efforts were in vain. "It's no use," said the doomed frog. "I'm stuck for good." Disheartened, his friends left him to his fate.

The next day the same friends came back, only to find the frog sitting beside the rut, croaking merrily. "What happened? We thought you couldn't get out!" exclaimed the friends.

"I couldn't," replied the frog. "But then a wagon came along and I *had* to!"

Desperation is the great motivator. Not simple discouragement but the real thing: gut-churning fear combined with the sure knowledge that it's too late to change your fate.

This chapter is an introduction to the people affected; to use an unflattering comparison, the frogs stuck in their ruts. These are the people whose lives you will be affecting profoundly. In many cases they'll see you as part of the machine trying to run them down. They may hate you long before they meet you.

We've been surprised at the reaction of many people facing foreclosure. They are often unwilling or unable to accept the reality of the sale, and they'll sit in their ruts until the very last moment, when they absolutely have to get out of the way or get run over.

As you learn about the process, you'll begin to understand their plight, and you'll learn the most vital lesson of all: foreclosure psychology. And if you really want to succeed you'll go one step further and learn how to empathize—not just sympathize—with their predicament.

CASE STUDY

To let you see the whole portrait of a foreclosure before we study the brush strokes, we'd like to introduce you to Gus and Doreen Johnson. Their story is as real as the book you're holding. The tragedy and personal heartbreak that you're going to read about actually happened and we were there to see it. We've changed enough details to shield the identities of all involved parties, but we've included copies of all the actual documents.

It's a story of pain and profit, failure and success. It's a tragic melodrama with a bittersweet ending. And, in our roles as the Dudley Do-rights, you'll see why we claim that foreclosure investors are heroes not villains.

The home that was involved had been in the Johnsons' family for three generations. Although it had been paid off 50 years before, Gus took out a first mortgage, based on the equity in the home, for $30,000 (actually, the home was worth $120,000, but he only needed the $30,000). His monthly payments were $408; well within his ability to repay—until the heart attack.

When Gus came home from the hospital, he came home to a stack of medical bills, a job he could no longer keep, and a

58

monthly mortgage payment he couldn't meet. He suddenly felt older than his 62 years. He felt like giving up.

The Johnsons missed their first payment in March, their second in April. Gus couldn't bring himself to explain to Doreen what had happened, and rather than face the truth he simply ignored the warnings from the bank.

The bank did what it had to do. It filed a notice of default. To assure you that this isn't a story made up to illustrate a point, take a look at the actual notice. This is a copy of the real thing (less some deletions to protect the owners' privacy) as it looked when Gus tore open the envelope.

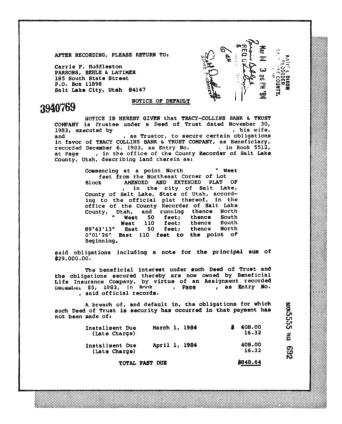

Gus began to see the seriousness of the problem, but like the frog stuck in the rut, he couldn't get out. He refused several offers, insisting that he get the full value for his property. He never contacted the bank, and he refused to work with investors or other interested buyers.

You should know by now what happened three months after the notice of default was filed. The trustee published a notice of sale.

NOTICE OF
TRUSTEE'S SALE
The following described property will be sold at public auction to the highest bidder on the 12th day of March, 1985, at 2:00 p.m. at the North door of the Courts Building, located between 200 and 300 East, on 400 South at Salt Lake City, Salt Lake County, Utah, for the purpose of foreclosing a Trust Deed executed by

, his wife, and

, as Trustor, TRACY-COLLINS BANK & TRUST COMPANY, Trustee, in favor of TRACY-COLLINS BANK & TRUST COMPANY, a Utah corporation, as Beneficiary, under the Trust Deed recorded December 6, as Entry No. , in Book at Page of the official records of Salt Lake County, State of Utah, given to secure an indebtedness in favor of TRACY-COLLINS BANK & TRUST COMPANY.

Notice of Default was recorded May 14, , as Entry No. , in Book at Page of said official records.

Trustee will sell at public auction to the highest bidder, in cash, payable in lawful money of the United States, at the time of sale, without warranty as to title, possession, or encumbrances, the following described property located in Salt Lake County, State of Utah, and more particularly described as follows:

Commencing at a point North West feet from the Northeast Corner of Lot 1, Block 8, AMENDED AND EXTENDED PLAT OF in the City of Salt Lake, County of Salt Lake, State of Utah, according to the official plat thereof, in the office of the County Recorder of Salt Lake County, Utah, and running thence North

West 50 feet; thence South 0°01'26" West 110 feet; thence South 89°43' 13" East 50 feet; thence North 0°01'26" East 110 feet to the point of Beginning.

For the purpose of paying obligations secured by said Trust Deed and including fees, charges, and expenses fo Trustee, and advances, if any, under the terms of said Trust Deed.

DATED this 7th day of February, 1985.
TRUSTEE:
TRACY-COLLINS BANK
& TRUST COMPANY
By Charles H. Madsen
Its Authorized Agent
Noel E. Chesley
PARSONS, BEHLE &
LATIMER
185 South State Street
P.O. Box 11898
Salt Lake City, Utah 84147
(2-15 3-1)

We didn't see the notice until its second publication, and by the time we reached Gus and Doreen the sale was only 10 days away. We knew that it meant working fast. We had only hours to convince Gus that he should sell his home to us.

Before we made an offer, however, we needed to know at least one important factor: how much equity was available. All we knew is that he was facing foreclosure. We had only a few days to find out how much the property was worth and how much was owed against it, including all liens, back payments, and legal fees.

We contacted the beneficiary and asked a few questions. The complete list will be found later in this chapter. We found that there were no other liens on the property. The balance of the foreclosed lien was $29,000. Including back payments and legal fees, the cost to acquire the property would be about $38,000. We added another $2,361 for holding costs (we figured we would own the property for no more than two months, and only minor repairs and maintenance would be required), giving us a total of $40,361 estimated purchasing costs.

On the selling end of the deal, we calculated that the appraised value of $124,000, minus all selling costs (Realtor's commissions, closing costs, attorney's fees, repairs, and a discount for quick sale), meant that we could gross $71,920 at the sale.

So we had a house that could be bought for $40,361 and sold for $71,920, which meant a net equity of $31,559 and that was a worst-case scenario. On the following page you can see our actual calculations. For us, it was a no-lose proposition.

You may have noticed something peculiar at the end of the form—our plan for distributing the equity. We were going to *give* Gus and Doreen $21,559! Think about it for a minute:

Analyzing a Transaction

1) Appraised Value: _124,000_

2) Selling Expenses:
   a. Realtor's commission (6%) _7,440_
   b. VA/FHA discount points (4%) _4,960_
   c. Closing cost (3%) _3,720_
   d. Stamp on deed, mortgage (1/2%) _620_
   e. Attorney's fee (1/2%) _620_
   f. Discount, incentive (9%) _(14%)_ _17,360_
   g. Misc. (repairs) (2-4%) _4,960_

   CRT. FIN. (10%) — 12,400 TOTAL COST _52,080_

3) Net Selling Price:
   Appraised Value _124,000_
   Minus Total Cost _-52,080_
   Equals Net Selling Price _71,920_

4) Determine Holding Costs:
   a. Monthly payments _454_
   b. Interest on money ⎫
   c. Utilities ⎬ 2361
   d. Insurance ⎪
   e. Repairs/maintenance ⎭
   f. Taxes

   TOTAL HOLDING _2,361_

5) Determine Purchasing Cost:
   a. Balance of mortgage(s) 30,000 + 6,000 _36,000_
   b. Balance of missed payments
   c. Balance of liens, judgments
   d. Legal fees and late charges ⎫
   e. Attorney's fees ⎬ approx
   f. Recording fee ⎪ 2000
   g. Assumption fee ⎭ _38,000_

   TOTAL PURCH.

6) Determine Total Absolute Cost:
   a. Purchase plus holding costs _40,361_

7) Determine Equity Available:
   Net Selling Price _71,920_
   (minus)
   Absolute Cost _40,361_
   (equals)
   Equity Available _31,559_

8) Solution: US: 10,000
   Note to Owner (minimize cash outlay) THEM: 21,559

They were going to lose their home anyway; the sale was as good as final. It was the last five minutes of the eleventh hour, and if they didn't accept whatever offer we threw at them they would lose everything. We could have offered them $2,000 for moving expenses and it would have been $2,000 more than the bank was going to give them. So why the generosity?

We've found—and mark this well—that we can make money without taking advantage of people. Furthermore, we've found that in doing so we have almost every offer accepted.

When we sat down with Gus at his kitchen table, we explained, as carefully and kindly as possible, that he was going to be evicted from his home in about two weeks. He had to understand that the time for naive optimism was passed. There would be no reprieve; the governor wasn't going to order a stay of execution. In less than two weeks an auction would be held and somebody—probably the bank— would be the new owner.

With Doreen in the other room, Gus changed from the intractable character we had first encountered to a broken man. With his last illusion destroyed, he broke down and wept. It was a pitifully touching sight. If only he could have seen the truth five or six months earlier! He could have sold the home for $90,000, paid off the $30,000 loan, and he would have had $60,000 with which to find a new home.

Our offer was considerably less than the $60,000 that he could have had, and we genuinely wished, for his sake, that he had sold his home earlier. But consider the alternatives: By the time we arrived on the scene it was too late for "what if's." He was either going to lose his home and be forced out without so much as $10 for gas money, or he would accept our offer and leave with over $20,000.

The predicament faced by Gus and Doreen wasn't one that we had created. We weren't the cause of their problem—we were the solution.

There are many people who confuse cause and effect. They suppose that foreclosure specialists are somehow responsible for the misfortunes they encounter. What a ridiculous notion! Consider this: You're driving down the highway when suddenly you see a car swerve and crash into a divider post. You pull over to the side and rush to the aid of the driver. His leg is broken, a compound fracture, which is bleeding profusely. It's too late to save the leg, so you tie a tourniquet. You've saved his life, but he's lost a leg. Is anyone going to accuse you of causing the accident? Will you be castigated because the leg was lost? Of course not. You'll be a hero.

The same thing happens with foreclosure investors. We see accidents. By the time we arrive on the scene it's usually too late to make everything all right. We can, however, save the financial lives of the victims—lives that would otherwise be lost in a foreclosure sale.

Investors aren't the cause of foreclosures, and people who criticize them for taking advantage of a bad situation should first consider the alternative. What would happen if there were no foreclosure investors? What would have happened to Gus and Doreen if we hadn't offered to buy their home and give them $21,000?

Gus and Doreen accepted our offer and thanked us for saving their financial life. We convinced a banker to lend us the necessary $70,000. We gave Gus and Doreen their $21,000 and gave them a month to find a new home. We paid off the $40,000 or so in debts against the property and immediately put it on the market, listing it through a real estate agent. It sold in less than two months for $85,000 and we cleared nearly $20,000 profit.

That's what foreclosure investing is all about.

The purpose of this chapter is to teach you how to find and recognize good foreclosure opportunities. How to solve someone else's problems and make money at the same time.

FINDING FORECLOSURES

You're about to begin the search. Your object is to find one property facing foreclosure; to determine whether or not it qualifies as a good deal; and, if it does, to buy it.

We'll start with the first part: finding foreclosures. We'll give you 10 methods for unearthing desperate sellers. By using a combination of two or three that look good to you, you shouldn't have trouble finding a good deal.

1) Lenders

Or, to be more precise, loan officers. When a loan is defaulted on, who is the first to know? Yes, of course the owner, but who else? Right, the lender.

If you can convince the lender to help you find good deals, you're ahead of the game. Once the notice of default is recorded, you will face competition and you'll be seen by the owners as another fin in the water.

That sounds great, doesn't it? You find a loan officer who will let you know the day someone goes into default and you immediately contact the owners and tie down the deal. Only one small problem: lenders won't tell you who is in default. Word could get out that they are telling tales out of school and they might find themselves at the end of the unemployment line.

But lenders can help. Occasionally you'll find one who is willing to "leak" a name or address, but better than that—or at least more ethical—is to have business cards made, announcing yourself as an interested buyer, and find a lender who will, as a courtesy to the owners in trouble, pass your card along. If the card is accompanied by a tactful letter, introducing yourself and stating that you are in the business of helping owners in trouble, you may be the first one called.

Large conventional lenders will often have a list of properties in foreclosure. These are properties for which a notice of default and a notice of sale have been recorded, so there is no problem with invading anyone's privacy. You should be able to get a copy of the list from the chief loan officer of any large savings and loan or bank.

2) Notices of Default

This source is obvious. Although NOD's aren't usually published in newspapers, like notices of sale, they are recorded in the county courthouse. Take an afternoon to explore the courthouse. In most counties you'll find patient personnel who will assist you in finding the notices.

Remember, the notice of default will contain a description of the property and the name of the trustor(s), the trustee, and the beneficiary. That will be enough to put you on the right track. You can contact any one of the three—or all three—to find out more about the property, as we'll discuss shortly. If there is only a legal description, and no street address, you can, as a last resort, dig it out of the county plat map (again, the staff should be able to help), but it's usually easier to talk to the beneficiary directly. Also, given the trustor's name, you can sometimes use the good old White Pages to find the street address.

3) Default Lists

Looking up notices of default is a time-consuming task. In its favor is the fact that you'll be ahead of investors who use only notices of sale. The only problem is that it's not only time consuming, but it's also often fruitless. You can spend hours chasing down deals that aren't good enough to waste your time on.

Nowadays, especially in large metropolitan areas, there are ten foreclosure investors for every good deal. As a result, companies have been formed that do nothing but compile and publish lists of properties facing foreclosure. You can buy their lists and save yourself hours in the courthouse.

4) Attorneys

This source is a lot like lenders. Lawyers are often consulted when someone is in financial trouble, so they make great contacts. Many people involved in divorces, bankruptcies, and probates are anxious to sell (whether there is a foreclosure involved or not), and a lawyer can refer you to them.

The problem with using lawyers is that, like lenders, they can't give out names and addresses of people who are in trouble without invading their privacy. Therefore, as with the lenders, we suggest that you use your business card or letter to introduce yourself. If the lawyer is convinced that you intend to act in the best interests of his or her client, you will be able to make contact.

5) Classified Ads (I)

Read the classified ads, under "Real estate for sale" at least a couple of nights a week. Many times an owner in trouble will place an ad that suggests desperation. It's not uncommon to see one that says, "Must Sell, will consider all offers." Some of them will be gimmicks to get you to call, but a few will be owners who have missed a payment or two and who really need your help.

6) Classified Ads (II)

Place an ad in the "Real estate wanted" column. It doesn't have to be fancy. It can be as simple as: "I will help you make up back payments," or "If you really need to sell, call me first." Investors who have used such ads report mixed results. If you can run them once or twice a week without paying a fortune, by all means do so. Your ad only has to pay off once or twice a year to be profitable.

7) Abandoned Homes

Ever drive past a house that was obviously left to the cats and the rats? Sometimes it's not so obvious; you might notice that the curtains are down and the rooms look empty, or the grass is getting out of hand.

Where there's an abandoned home there's a trustor in trouble—if the property hasn't already been repossessed by the bank. Actually there are three possibilities: The owners are making long-distance payments. They have given up and the bank is taking a beating, waiting to sell the property. Or the sale has already taken place and a new owner—usually the lender—is stuck with an unsalable eyesore.

No matter what stage of crisis it's in, you can come to the rescue. The first chore is to find the owners. Leave a note on the door, asking the current owners to get in touch if they are interested in selling. Fill out a request for change of address information at the local post office. Ask the county tax assessor for the most recent address of the owners.

If you do find the owners, chances are very good that they'll be eager to sell. Nine times out of ten the home will either be somewhere in the process of foreclosure or will have already been sold. The tenth house will have an owner who is still trying to make the payments, and it's unlikely that owner will turn down a chance to sell the monkey on his back.

If the property is owned by the lender (bank, savings and loan, FHA, VA, "Fannie Mae," etc.) you can probably still get a good deal. We'll cover that situation in detail in a later chapter. What we're looking for in this chapter is an owner who has abandoned the property but hasn't lost it yet.

8) Realtors

Let's stop for another vocabulary lesson. A *Realtor* (always capitalized) is a real estate agent or broker who is a member of the National Association of Realtors. A non-Realtor agent has earned the state's license to sell real estate, but a Realtor has additionally passed the more stringent requirements of the NAR. Therefore we recommend Realtors over non-Realtor agents, and we use the term Realtor throughout the book. However, we offer the recommendation with a caveat: a knowledgable, hard-working non-Realtor agent is worth a hundred lazy Realtors.

Realtors are a good source of information. They are in contact with a wide range of sellers, and they are often the first to be called in times of crisis. Through the Multiple Listing Service, wherein all of the Realtors in a specific area can pool their homes for sale, any agent can put you in touch with hundreds of sellers.

A poor Realtor is about as useless as an appendicitis. That is, they serve no useful purpose, and they can be a real pain in the side. A good Realtor, on the other hand, can locate the best deals on the market: foreclosures in the making. When home owners miss a couple of payments, and receive nasty letters from the lender, they know they are in trouble. If relief is nowhere in sight, they may face the truth—that they are going to lose their home—and call a Realtor. If you have developed a good relationship with at least one on-the-ball Realtor, who will get the first call? Keep in mind the fact that it is a Realtor's job to find buyers for these anxious sellers. They don't take great pleasure in showing the same house to dozens of potential buyers, and if they know one motivated investor (guess who?), they will let their fingers do some fast walking.

Finding a good Realtor isn't always easy. Every city in the U.S. has more than its share of agents, and many of them are lackadaisical in their work, making just enough in commissions to meet their bills.

Also, Realtors are often wary of working with investors. They know that investors are always looking for good deals and that means low commissions and hard-to-please buyers. Furthermore, Realtors have a financial responsibility to their clients. That is, they cannot jeopardize the client's interests by letting prospective buyers know that they are desperate to sell.

The answer is to develop a close working relationship with one Realtor whom you feel comfortable working with. If you have a great property for sale, let your Realtor list it. Once you've worked together on a couple of deals, you'll be the first one called when a choice property becomes available.

Actually, Realtors, lawyers and lenders are only the beginning of your connections. You can spread the word at work, at church, on community bulletin boards. Any social situation is a chance to let people know you buy real estate. You don't have to mention the fact that you specialize in foreclosure properties. And, of course, you really don't have to specialize in foreclosures to make money. Just let everyone know that you're interested in finding good deals. After a while your reputation will spread.

9) Shotgun Letters
So called because they work like shotgun pellets, these are

letters that you send out to every owner of property in any stage of foreclosure. Your letter should be a general, "I buy real estate" kind of letter. You don't need to mention the foreclosure—they are already too aware of the situation and don't need a reminder.

Every time you find a home in default, fire off a letter. One in ten will respond, and one in ten responses will put you in touch with a good deal. That means about 100 letters for one solid connection, but like the "I'll buy your house" ad in the paper, it doesn't have to pay off every time to be profitable.

An alternative to the shotgun letter is the leaflet or flyer. You can make up a single-page flyer saying "I Buy Houses," that encourages sellers to contact you first. You can leave one of your flyers at the door of every foreclosure property in town and wait for a response.

As with the letter, 99 out of 100 flyers will find themselves at the bottom of the bird cage, but the hundredth one will be a winner.

10) Notice of Sale

You should have seen this one coming. We saved the most obvious—and the easiest, if not always the best—for last. Finding foreclosure properties through the NOS's is by far the armchair investor's best method. It only takes a few minutes each night to glance through the notices in your local paper (which we suggest subscribing to), and by contacting the beneficiary, the trustee, or the trustor you can find out all you need to know about the property.

There are three major drawbacks to this method, and you can't get around them. The first is that notices of sale will be published on *all* properties going into foreclosure, not just the pick of the crop. You may find yourself chasing after homes that you wouldn't want to buy anyway—homes overburdened with debt, homes in bad areas of town, homes that are too big, too small, too run down, too . . . you name it.

The second obstacle is that by the time the notice of sale is published, the foreclosure has already been a matter of public record for months—plenty of time for the rest of the flock to have descended. Many of the best foreclosure opportunities have already been bought up long before they reach the NOS stage.

The third difficulty is the fact that even if you catch the first publication of the NOS, you only have a few weeks to put your offer together, get it accepted and financed and closed. It doesn't leave a lot of time for leisurely contemplation; you've got to be ready to move.

None of these problems means an end to your hope of finding that perfect money machine. Like our experience with the Johnsons, there will always be a few good deals waiting to be found only hours before the auction, and a quick witted investor will be able to make a fortune by finding one every couple of months.

FINDING OUT ABOUT THE DEAL

Finding a property in foreclosure isn't a tough proposition; with the highest foreclosure rates in the history of real estate, there's practically one on every street corner. But that doesn't mean they are all great deals.

There are three stages in a foreclosure when you can purchase the property: before, during, and after the sale. Which time is the best time to buy depends mostly on the financing—if it's advantageous to buy at all.

To decide whether or not a house is worth buying, you should take three things—location, market value, and financing—into consideration. Location, because a home in a run-down neighborhood is rarely a good deal. A neglected home in a good neighborhood can usually be fixed up and sold at a profit. But the same home in a low-grade area may be impossible to sell no matter how much fix-up money and sales efforts you pour into it.

Before we go on to market value and financing, let's stop and put what you've learned so far into perspective. We'll say that you've begun your search. You've used one of the methods described above to find a property in some stage of the foreclosure process. You've determined that it isn't in a substandard area (we recommend three- or four-bedroom homes in solid blue-collar neighborhoods). If you're with us so far, you're ready for your next step: determining current market value or at least a fairly accurate estimate of market value.

By definition, market value is the price at which anything will sell, given a reasonable selling period. In real estate, reasonable is three to six months. If the three-bedroom down the block will take a year to sell at $85,000, six months to sell at $75,000, and two weeks to sell at $65,000, its true market value is about $75,000. When someone loses money on a "sure thing" real estate deal because they can't sell it at the price they had anticipated, chances are better than good that they miscalculated market value.

The true test of market value is what a particular piece of property sells for, period. If real estate was a perfect market, determining market value would be a piece of cake. Everyone would agree that Jim and Betty's house on Elm Street was worth $85,000, and that would be the end of it.

Unfortunately, that isn't the way it works on the real Elm Street. Jim thinks his house is worth $95,000; Frank sold his for $90,000 last month, and his didn't even have an open pit grill like the one Jim put in the back yard! Betty thinks the house is absolutely priceless; it was from that very front door she sent Jim Junior off to his first day at school. The prospective buyers walking through aren't about to pay more than $80,000—they hate that awful pit in the back yard.

So how can you, as a novice foreclosure expert, drive by a house and determine its value? You can't. It's that simple. It will take months before you can look at any house on any block in your city and give it a rough appraisal. However, there are a few tricks you can use as you learn prices.

Realtors

Everywhere you turn in this business you're back to working with the Realtor. And with good reason: the more you work with a good Realtor the more you'll treasure this source of knowledge and advice.

It's a Realtor's job to be familiar with the price of homes in an area. You should have already found at least one that you can call up and ask for a quick appraisal. Offer an incentive—$25 or so—for an educated guess. (We hope that you've chosen an experienced Realtor whose guess will be very educated.) Ask your Realtor friend for old copies of MLS books. These books list homes for sale, along with their prices. Drive by the homes listed and take a good look; familiarize yourself with market values as quickly as possible. The education will save both time and money.

Comparables

One appraisal method used by professional appraisers is the market comparison method. In theory, if three identical houses situated in the same neighborhood all sell for the same price, a fourth identical house in the same neighborhood will sell for that price also. The logic is inarguable. Unfortunately, no such neighborhood exists. However, you can do quite well by driving through a neighborhood and finding three houses similar to your object property that have "For Sale" signs staked to their lawns. Call the numbers listed on the signs (realty offices) and ask the selling price of the comparable properties. If the first is selling for $67,000, the second for $68,000, and the third for $71,000, you at least have a price range to work with.

Tax Records

Here again you have an opportunity to put those public records—the ones you never knew you had access to—to work. Property tax assessment records are on file with the county. Visit the county courthouse and ask for assistance. Taxes are based on a property's assessed value, by a simple formula your Realtor or title officer can help you figure out. Working with the formula, you know that if taxes on a particular home were $6,200, then the assessed value of the home was $72,500 (using purely hypothetical numbers).

Perhaps the most important thing at this point is to avoid getting bogged down in details. You only need a rough idea of the property's market value to know whether or not it is worthwhile. Many beginning investors, afraid of making a mistake, analyze a property to death and never make an offer. If you know the house is worth somewhere between $80,000 and $90,000, and you also know it has one lien against it for $45,000, do you need someone to tell you it's a good deal? There is a lot of equity packed into that house, and if the owners are six months behind in their payments with no hope in sight, will they give up a good share of that equity? In most cases, yes.

Another recap: You've found and looked at the property (or at least you've driven by to check out the house and the area), you've assured yourself that it's in a good location and in relatively good condition (it might need minor cosmetic repairs), and you've determined its approximate market value. Now what?

FINANCING HISTORY

It's time to find out about the financing. You've got to know how many liens are leaning and how many mortgages are . . . uh, mortgaging. There are three sources:

□ Trustors (owners)
□ Beneficiary (lender)
□ Trustee.

Let's start with the lenders, who will be in the best position to answer questions—and to help you avoid tangling with obstinate owners.

You won't have any trouble finding the lender's name; it will appear in the notice of default and the notice of sale. When you call a commercial lender, ask to speak to the loan officer in charge of foreclosures.

Sometimes loan officers will be unwilling to help, which is a strange response, since it is in the bank's best interest to avoid foreclosures. They may really have something against investors, or more likely, they may simply be unable to disclose specific facts about the financing without the permission of the owner. You'll find, however, that most loan officers are happy to help once you've proven to them that you are a professional who is there to help.

The accompanying questionnaire should make it easy to get the facts you'll need.

After the lender, the next one to approach is the owner. You'll find that owners fall into two very distinct categories: those who are willing to work with you and those who will wish you in hell without a glass of ice water. From the first you will get all kinds of valuable information; from the

---

Questionnaire for Lenders

1) Who holds the Fee Title?
2) Who holds the Equitable Title? (Applicable when a real estate contract is involved.)
3) Is there a divorce involved?
4) Are there any equitable liens against the property?
5) What has the owner said about the foreclosure?
6) Do you think the owner will be receptive to a foreclosure specialist?
7) Have you asked for a deed in lieu of foreclosure?
8) Has the owner offered to deed the property to you?
9) Do you know if the property is listed?
10) Do you know if the owner is living at the property?
11) Could you please tell me what the appraisal was at the time the loan was made?
12) Do you have a newer appraisal?
13) What type of loan are you foreclosing? (VA, FHA, conventional, etc.)
14) What is the current balance on the loan?
15) What are the monthly payments? Do they include a reserve for taxes and insurance?
16) How much money will be required to bring the loan current, not counting trustee's fees and costs?

---

second you won't get the time of day.

The loan officer responsible for a specific loan will usually know the owner's state of mind and can prepare you ahead of time. If the owner is unapproachable, you may have to turn to the trustee for more answers and leave the owner for last— like one week before the sale.

If the owner is anxious to sell, you should be able to get all of your questions answered. Use the form on the next page.

Now, in addition to whatever information you were able to obtain from the lender, you have the owner's opinion of the property's value, the asking price, the loan information, all of the lenders' names and phone numbers (not just the one

Questionnaire for Home Owners

1. Name _____
2. Address _____
3. Asking Price $ _____
4. How was price determined?
5. First Mortgage:
   - Balance $ _____
   - Payments $ _____
   - # of missed payments _____
   - Total of missed payments $ _____
   - Type of Loan (FHA, VA, etc.)
   - Is loan assumable? _____
   - Interest rate _____
   - Lender _____
   - Lender's phone number _____
6. Second Mortgage:
   - Balance $ _____
   - Payments $ _____
   - # of missed payments _____
   - Total of missed payments $ _____
   - Type of Loan (FHA, VA, etc.) _____
   - Is loan assumable? _____
   - Interest rate _____
   - Lender _____
   - Lender's phone number _____
7. Third Mortgage:
   - Balance $ _____
   - Payments $ _____
   - # of missed payments _____
   - Total of missed payments $ _____
   - Type of Loan (FHA, VA, etc.) _____
   - Is loan assumable? _____
   - Interest rate _____
   - Lender _____
   - Lender's phone number _____
8. Late Charges and Legal Fees incurred $ _____
9. Total Debt (add 5 through 8) $ _____

OWNER'S STATED EQUITY: $ _____
   - Asking Price $ _____
   - Less Total Debt $ _____
   - Owner's Equity $ _____
   - Terms (As stated by seller)

_____
_____
_____
_____

foreclosing), and other pertinent facts.

Keep in mind, when talking to owners, that they'll always want top dollar for their homes. If they can find someone who'll pay their asking price, great. If they can't, then they will come back to you before the sale. Don't feel pressured at this point to agree to unprofitable terms.

If the owner isn't willing to discuss selling—or at least isn't willing to discuss it with some "no-good investor," you'll have to turn to the last one on your list: the trustee.

Trustees come in all shapes and sizes. Some of the larger lending institutions have their own in-house trustee departments. Others use professional trustees. Some use attorneys. The qualifications for trustees vary from state to state, so the trustee involved may be anyone from a private citizen to a giant corporation.

Trustees don't like to be called on to provide specific information. Most of them will refer you back to the benefici-

---

Questionnaire for Trustees

1) Who holds the Fee Title?
2) Who holds the Equitable Title?
3) Are there any equitable liens granted by a divorce decree?
4) What are the other liens against the property?
5) Did the owner receive the NDF sent to him by registered mail?
6) At what address did the owner receive the NDF (if you haven't been able to find them)?
7) Have you received any phone calls from other claimants concerning a reinstatement or payoff?
8) What has the owner said about the foreclosure?
9) How much money will be required to bring the loan current, plus all fees and costs?
10) What is the current loan balance?
11) What are the monthly payments? Do they include a reserve for taxes and insurance?
12) What individual at the lending institution would be the most knowledgeable about this particular loan and this particular borrower?

---

ary or to the owner and will refuse to give details or advice. If you can find a trustee who will cooperate, you can ask many of the same questions that you asked the beneficiary.

With the information gleaned from the big three, you should be able to decide whether or not the deal is worth pursuing. To put it all together, let's use an example:

The house is a six-year-old three-bedroom rambler in a good area. All you know about it is that similar homes in the same area are selling for $94,000.

Situation 1

There are three liens against it. The first mortgage has an outstanding balance of $45,500 with payments of $525. It is on the first mortgage that the owners are four months behind. This is the foreclosing beneficiary. The balance on the second mortgage is $35,400, with payments of $420. The owners are three months behind in their payments. The third mortgage has a balance of $25,000. They are three months behind on payments of $295.

Would it be a good idea to buy this house from the owner, before the foreclosure sale? Think about it before answering.

If you said yes, you haven't been paying attention. Come down to the front of the class where we can keep an eye on you. Consider the facts:

The total outstanding loans equal $105,900—over $10,000 more than the property is worth! This can easily be the case when prices are falling, especially if any of the liens are graduated payment mortgages with reverse amortization, where the loan balance increases the first few years.

No matter what kind of deal you cut with the owners, you'll be saddled with the $105,900 debt, and back payments of $4,245, plus legal fees and closing costs, for a total well over $110,000.

You'd be crazy, if you'll excuse our bluntness, to buy directly from the owner.

Your best bet would be to either buy at the auction or from the new owner (probably one of the lienholders) after the auction. We'll discuss these options in more detail in a later chapter. For now all you need to know is that this isn't a great opportunity for buying directly from the owner.

Situation 2

There is only one lien against the property, a first mortgage for $45,000. The sale is three weeks away and the owners have rejected all offers as being too low. They are six months behind in their payments of $445 (sound familiar?).

Should you make an offer to the owners?

If so, for how much? No, don't read the answer yet. Work it out.

The first answer is easy. Yes, it would probably be advantageous to make an offer. The back payments total $2,670. Added to the balance on the mortgage, the total debt is $47,670. Throw in a couple thousand more for legal fees, recording and closing costs, and the least you could get the property for is about $50,000. You know you can sell it for $90,000, and it will sell in less than a month at $85,000. If you can convince the owners that they are really going to lose their home, you're sure you can buy it for $70,000 (giving them about $20,000 more than they will get if it goes to sale) and clear $15,000 profit. It looks like an excellent foreclosure opportunity.

To make all of these calculations easier, use the form on the following page. Does the form look familiar? It's the same one we used when we purchased the Johnson's home under similar circumstances. Let's actually use the form to

Analyzing a Transaction

1) Appraised Value: _____

2) Selling Expenses:
   a. Realtor's commission (6%) _____
   b. VA/FHA discount points (4%) _____
   c. Closing cost (3%) _____
   d. Stamp on deed, mortgage (1/2%) _____
   e. Attorney's fee (1/2%) _____
   f. Discount, incentive (9%) _____
   g. Misc. (repairs) (2-4%) _____

   TOTAL COST _____

3) Net Selling Price:
   Appraised Value _____
   Minus Total Cost _____
   Equals Net Selling Price _____

4) Determine Holding Costs:
   a. Monthly payments _____
   b. Interest on money _____
   c. Utilities _____
   d. Insurance _____
   e. Repairs/maintenance _____
   f. Taxes _____

   TOTAL HOLDING _____

5) Determine Purchasing Cost:
   a. Balance of mortgage(s) _____
   b. Balance of missed payments _____
   c. Balance of liens, judgments _____
   d. Legal fees and late charges _____
   e. Attorney's fees _____
   f. Recording fee _____
   g. Assumption fee _____

   TOTAL PURCH. _____

6) Determine Total Absolute Cost:
   a. Purchase plus holding costs _____

7) Determine Equity Available:
   Net Selling Price _____
      (minus)
   Absolute Cost _____
      (equals)
   Equity Available _____

8) Solution:
   Note to Owner (minimize cash outlay)

analyze our example, using best-guess estimates for all factors. Keep in mind that this is a worst-case scenario; we fully expect that the profit picture will be better than we're painting it here, but we don't want to take any chances.

Let's stop here for a second and figure out what we've done. What we're trying to do so far is determine how much money we'll have left on the table after we've sold the property. We've agreed to discount the selling price to $85,000 for a quick sale, and we've had to pay out several expenses including closing costs, FHA points, and Realtor's commissions. What we're left with is $70,120—quite a discount from the selling price of $85,000 and a far cry from the market value of $92,000.

The next step is to determine more precisely how much it's going to cost to buy the house. Ooops! Something funny happened on the way to making a fortune on this deal. It all sounded so good at first: We'd buy it for $70,000, sell it for $85,000, and clear $15,000. Now it's apparent that if we buy it for $70,000 we'll make $120!

That's the value of having this form to help you take every factor into consideration. There's really only $16,895 equity available, after all expenses. If you give the owners $10,000 walking money—only half what you were originally planning—you'll only make $6,895. Now, that's not a bad wage for a month's part-time work, but it's not the fortune you had envisioned.

Actually, as we've said several times, this is a worst-case scenario. Many of the factors, such as FHA points and Realtor's commissions can be avoided (the first by restricting the buyer from FHA financing; the second by selling the property without the help of a Realtor). Other costs were purposely overestimated. Nevertheless, it's a good object lesson in not counting your chicks before you see the whites

Analyzing a Transaction

1) Appraised Value: <u>$92,000</u>

2) Selling Expenses:
   - a. Realtor's commission (6%)*   <u>$ 5,520</u>
   - b. VA/FHA discount points (4%)**   <u>3,680</u>
   - c. Closing cost (3%)   <u>2,760</u>
   - d. Stamp on deed, mortgage (1/2%)   <u>460</u>
   - e. Attorney's fee (1/2%)   <u>460</u>
   - f. Discount, incentive (9%)   <u>7,000</u>
   - g. Misc. (repairs) (2-4%)   <u>2,000</u>

                          TOTAL COST   <u>21,880</u>

3) Net Selling Price:
   - Appraised Value   <u>$92,000</u>
   - Minus Total Cost   <u>21,880</u>
   - Equals Net Selling Price   <u>$70,120</u>

4) Determine Holding Costs:
   - a. Monthly payments   <u>$ 445***</u>
   - b. Interest on money   _____
   - c. Utilities   _____
   - d. Insurance   _____
   - e. Repairs/maintenance   _____
   - f. Taxes   <u>2,000****</u>

                          TOTAL HOLDING   <u>2,445</u>

5) Determine Purchasing Cost:
   - a. Balance of mortgage(s)   <u>$45,000</u>
   - b. Balance of missed payments   <u>2,670</u>
   - c. Balance of liens, judgments   _____
   - d. Legal fees and late charges   <u>500</u>
   - e. Attorney's fees   <u>500</u>
   - f. Recording fee   <u>1,000</u>
   - g. Assumption fee   <u>1,110</u>

                          TOTAL PURCH.   <u>50,780</u>

(cont.)

6) Determine Total Absolute Cost:
    a. Purchase plus holding costs $53,225

7) Determine Equity Available:
    Net Selling Price $70,120

     (minus)
Absolute Cost   53,225

     (equals)
Equity Available $16,895

8) Solution:
    Note to Owner (minimize cash outlay)

    *We may not use a Realtor when we sell; if not, we don't need to include this factor.

    **If the buyer uses FHA or VA financing, we, the sellers, will have to pay some of the discount points. It's a strange way to do business, but it's a government program, so what can you expect?

    ***We're assuming that we'll own the property for two months, in spite of the fact that we're fairly confident we can sell it in less than a month. It's a case of better safe than sorry.

    ****We're lumping (b) through (f) together for simplicity's sake. You would have to ask the owner for specific numbers if this were a real case.

of their yolks, to scramble an old saying.

If the numbers add up to a profitable deal (this one looks good, if you can keep those costs down and convince the owners to take only $10,000 for their equity), then make your offer. The worst they can do is say no. And who knows? They might say yes . . . and you'll be a few thousand dollars richer.

A second form that we've designed will serve as a back-up analysis. It will allow you to take the information garnered thus far and put it through a Buy or Pass sifter. Not coincidentally, we call it the "To Buy or Pass" form.

If the bottom line from both forms points to enough equity available before foreclosure to make the deal profitable, by all means negotiate with the seller before it's too late.

In many cases there won't be enough equity to make working with the owners feasible.

When you have determined which situation exists, you

To Buy or Pass?

Address: _____

Owner: _____

Market value: Normal _____

                  Quick _____

Cash to reinstate 1st	_____
Cash to bring current	_____
Pay off	_____
Balance	_____
Cash to reinstate 2nd	_____
Cash to bring current	_____
Pay off	_____
Balance	_____
Cash to reinstate 3rd	_____
Cash to bring current	_____
Pay off	_____
Balance	_____
Judgments	_____
	_____
	_____
Mechanic liens	_____
	_____
Delinquent property taxes	_____
Federal tax liens	_____
Total encumbrances	_____
Max. available equity	_____
Cash to owner	_____
Maximum equity	_____

should be able to chart a course of action. If the property is relatively clean (only one or two liens against it), and there is instant equity available, buy it yesterday. If, however, it is dirty, you may have to let it pass through the trustee's sale before you touch it.

If there is little or no equity now, because of third, fourth, fifth liens, you may simply want to show up at the sale and make your bid. If the first or second mortgage holder is foreclosing, the junior claimants may be willing to sell their positions to you at a substantial discount, or they may not show up for the sale. If they don't show up, they will be wiped out at the time of the sale, freeing up extra equity that you can buy.

Your Fortune in Foreclosures Flowchart

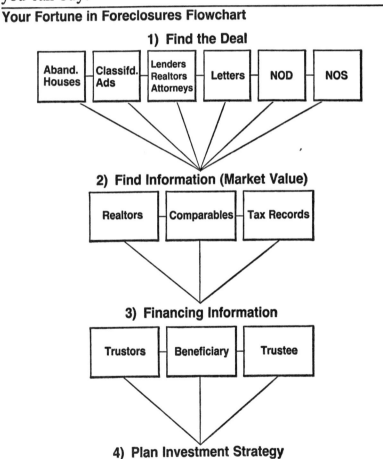

1) Find the Deal

| Aband. Houses | Classifd. Ads | Lenders Realtors Attorneys | Letters | NOD | NOS |

2) Find Information (Market Value)

| Realtors | Comparables | Tax Records |

3) Financing Information

| Trustors | Beneficiary | Trustee |

4) Plan Investment Strategy

Let's review briefly before we go to meet the owners face to face. The flowchart on the previous page shows the ground we've covered so far.

You can see from the flowchart that you already know enough now to find a property in foreclosure and to track down the details you need to determine whether or not it's a good deal. If you'll spend an hour or two each night and a couple of Saturdays each month finding and analyzing foreclosure properties, it shouldn't take more than a month or two to find one that will work.

Now comes the tough part: planning your strategy and making an actual offer.

To buy from the owners you'll have to apply equal amounts of psychology and financial analysis—and we'll cover both in the next chapter.

CHAPTER FOUR

Buying Before The Sale: Planning & Negotiating

We'll start this chapter with a few basic assumptions:

□ You have followed the program so far and found a property facing foreclosure.

□ You have contacted the lender, the owner, and possibly the trustee, so you have a clear picture of the existing financing.

□ You have at least a rough idea of the property's market value.

□ You have completed the transaction analysis form and you've determined that there is enough equity available to make a profit. (If there isn't enough equity you can still make money, as we'll see in the next two chapters.)

□ You've decided to buy the property from the owner, rather than wait and buy at or after the trustee's sale.

□ You're still reading this book.

WHY NOT BUY AT AUCTION?

There may be a couple of questions on your mind at this point: If there is so much instant equity involved in an auction, why go to the trouble of negotiating with an owner?

If this book's purpose is to teach you how to buy foreclosure properties, why are we spending so much time teaching you how to buy before the trustee's sale? There are three reasons: cash, risk, and price.

Cash

The highest bidder at a trustee's sale, in most instances, must pay for the property with cash or a cashier's check. If you have that kind of money under your mattress, buying at auction may be the best way to go. However, most people don't have the money on hand, and they don't have enough time or credit to secure a quick-cash loan.

Even if the cash is available, it is often a better idea to work with the seller and buy a $10,000 equity with $2,000 cash, rather than showing up at auction and risking $50,000 cash for the same $10,000 return.

Risk

Many times an investor will find out about a sale only by reading a notice of sale a few days beforehand. Without the opportunity to inspect and appraise the property, the investor is buying blind equity with possibly hidden senior liens. The risk may or may not pay off.

Price

When working with an owner, you can control the terms of the deal. You can negotiate the price. At auction you lose that control, unless you are the only bidder (besides the beneficiary of the foreclosure). When there is substantial equity to be bought, there will often be competition. Other bidders may drive the price beyond your range, and you will lose the deal you could have consummated with the owner.

Our advice is that if there is enough equity available to

make it worthwhile, always work with the owners.

FIRST STEP: FORMULATE AN INVESTMENT PLAN

At this point you should be ready to formulate a plan, if not make a written offer. A tentative plan is obviously necessary before you get into negotiations with the owners. How you'll structure the offer will depend on many factors including:

☐ The cash needed to close the deal;

☐ The available financing;

☐ The time left before the auction;

☐ How long you plan to hold the property;

☐ The willingness of the owner to negotiate.

Because each situation is unique, we can't design a business plan that will work every time. You'll have to become familiar with loan officers, title officers, Realtors, the laws in your state, and you should know what loan packages are available. We'll cover each of these, and more, in this chapter, but only in general terms.

An important thing to realize at this juncture is that your investing activity is no longer linear. Up until now it's been step one, step two, step three, etc. Now as you lay out your grand plan you'll have to work with several factors at once, and each factor will depend on and influence the others. To formulate an integrated plan, you'll have to take all of the various elements into account.

We can break those elements into three basic categories: money, time, and the owner. Money includes both the down payment (if any) and mortgage financing; time means how much time it will take to buy the property, versus how much time before it's too late; and the owner is the wild-card factor who will influence both your time and money calculations.

MONEY

There's an old saying: It takes money to make money. And there's a modified version of the same saying, as it applies to real estate: It takes money to make money—but it doesn't have to be *your* money.

In almost every real estate transaction the money will be divided into two distinct categories: cash and financing. Cash includes the down payment, closing costs, delinquent payments, attorney's fees, carrying costs, fix-up costs—in short, any out-of-pocket expense incurred, and paid, by the buyer. Financing is simply how much you'll owe after paying the cash costs, and how you intend to pay for it.

Cash

One of your first priorities is determining the cash-to-acquire factor. How much money—cash money—will you need to buy the property?

Finding a good deal isn't enough; you must be able to afford what you find. Simply knowing you can make $10,000 on a single transaction won't provide you with the cash to close the deal—but it can help. If a house has a quick-sale value of $60,000, and you know you can buy it for $45,000, you can probably find someone ready and eager to buy it from you the minute it falls into your hands.

If, on the other hand, you will be keeping your property for a while, as a rental, you're stuck with the problem of paying the past, present and future bills. Such bills may include:

□ The owner's equity.
□ Trustee's fees.
□ Delinquent payments and accrued interest charges.
□ Delinquent property taxes.
□ Current property taxes.
□ Title policy costs and closing fees.

- Assumption fees for all loans.
- Judgments.
- Mechanic liens.
- Fire and liability insurance.
- Loan payments until property is rented.
- Refurbishing costs.
- Utility bills—prior and current.
- Relocation expense of prior owner.
  . . . to name a few.

The amount of cash involved here could easily pay for a day at Disneyland for the entire Osmond family. Estimating the cash needed will require some careful planning. The cash analysis sheet on the next page should help.

Where to Find Cash

Once you've determined how much cash you need, you face a second challenge: how to get it. Unless you can structure a "nothing-down" deal, you're going to have to come up with the cash if you want to buy the property. And if that cash isn't already sitting in your bank account, you'll have to borrow it.

Somewhere in America, it happens almost every day, an investor stumbles onto an owner who jumps at the chance to be rid of his $90,000 headache. He's aware that there's $40,000 equity, but he's two months behind already, with a third payment staring him in the face and no chance to catch up, and he's ready to go back to being a renter. The investor ties up the house with a $100 deposit, finds a buyer willing to buy the contract for half the equity right away, and walks away with a cool $20,000—without ever having to own the property. It's the ultimate nothing-down deal.

This also happens almost every day: A gambler puts three shiny silver dollars into the big machine in the lobby of a Las

---

Cash to Acquire

Address: _____

Owner: _____

Market Value: _____

1st mortgage:

    Cash to reinstate   _____

    Cash to bring current   _____

    Cash to carry for _____ months _____

2nd mortgage:

    Cash to reinstate   _____

    Cash to bring current   _____

    Cash to carry for _____ months _____

3rd mortgage:

    Cash to reinstate   _____

    Cash to bring current   _____

    Cash to carry for _____ months _____

Cash to owner*

(including relocation) _____

Cash for title policy & closing _____

Cash for assumption fees _____

Cash to pay judgments _____

Cash to pay mechanic liens _____

Cash for current taxes and insurance _____

Cash for delinquent taxes _____

Cash for refurbishing _____

Cash for miscellaneous expenses _____

Total Cash _____

Total maximum equity _____

*Only cash required to buy property.

Vegas casino and pulls the handle. The bars fall into place and bingo! He's $20,000 richer, just like that.

The truth is, jackpots are few and far between. Ninety-nine times out of a hundred you'll need more than $100 to make your profit. Analysis forms such as the one just shown are great . . . until you fill them out and discover you need about twice as much cash as you have in the old savings account.

So let's say you've done your homework and you know how much cash you'll need beyond what you can borrow from a mortgage broker. If your savings come up short, you'll have to solve the problem by either taking on an investment partner or borrowing the cash from a third party.

Investment Partners

If you don't have the money, somebody else does. Forming a partnership may seem like a formidable task, until you actually try it. The surprise is how easily it can be done. If you have already laid the groundwork for a deal that shows potential for high profits, finding a partner won't be difficult. Use the forms you've been given in this book to show your prospective partners exactly what they will be getting for their money.

Before forming a partnership—even before approaching a prospective partner—decide exactly how the profits and responsibilities are to be divided. If you are just getting started, and you are very cash poor, you can offer to do all of the research, all of the legwork, all of the fixing up, the renting, the advertising and the selling. All you're asking for is financial support. If you can prove to potential partners that the investment under consideration will return ten times their money in six months, how difficult will it be to find a willing backer?

Who should you have as a partner? Anyone with enough

money to finance your venture. Friend, relative, banker, Realtor, lawyer, your plumber.

One of the best sources of partners is a local investment group. Such a group will often include a few investors who have the money but not the time for active investing. They will quickly grasp the mechanics involved when you show them a potential gold mine.

When you've targeted several possible partners, put together a comprehensive, well-coordinated report that details your intended investment. Type it on clean paper. Don't scrawl it out with an old Bic on dog-eared Peanuts stationery.

An impressive-looking investment analysis, accompanied by a business card and a cover letter, all bound in a report folder, should attract enough potential partners that you'll spend most of your time fighting them off. Send a copy to anyone you know who might have the money to invest. Give them three or four days to respond, and include a note to the effect that if they are not interested in this particular investment, they may request to be put on your list for consideration in future ventures.

If you don't get an immediate response, analyze your investment again. Are you offering enough return? How are profits to be split? How much profit have you projected, and how have you supported those projections? Uncle Harry won't part easily with his $20,000 if you are only projecting a $2,000 return over the next six months, based on half-researched possible rental rates. But $5,000 instant equity and a total after-tax profit of $8,000, based on thoroughly researched projections, and old Uncle Harry will whip out a pen and a checkbook so fast it'll make your eyes water.

When you do find a partner who is at least willing to discuss terms with you, be prepared. Have all of the information about the property at your fingertips, neatly filed. Have a partnership agreement worked out in advance, with an attorney. Even the best partnerships run into occasional problems, and a verbal partnership agreement with even a minor snag can lead to troubles.

You and your partner should take title to the property as tenants in common. In that case, you will both own 50% of the property and if either of you should die, your share will pass into your estate for your heirs to squabble over.

You may form a limited partnership or a general partnership. A limited partnership agreement must be filed with the clerk of the district court; a general partnership does not have to be filed. In either case, have a qualified attorney's advice before you form any partnership.

If you take title to the property using your own names, you won't have trouble with title insurance. However, if you elect to use a trade name, such as "Equity Builders," and if you have not filed your partnership agreement with the lieutenant governor/secretary of state, you will probably run into trouble. The title company won't know who *all* the partners are, who is authorized to sign for the partnership, and what limits the partners have imposed on themselves.

A partnership is often the best solution to the cash problem. It avoids the hassles involved in borrowing from a conventional lender, and your partner will be there every step of the way, boosting your morale and encouraging your success.

Friends and Relatives

If you have to borrow the down payment, and you can't find a partner, you may find yourself turning to friends or family. They can lend you the money, but if you're planning on borrowing the balance of the purchase money from an institutional lender you'll have to get a "gift letter" from your benefactor, in which he certifies *that the money is a gift, not a loan.*

A strong warning is in order here. Do not use the gift-letter loan unless your lender understands that you are not legally liable to repay the money. It's much better to borrow the money with an agreement to repay it beginning in some future year than it is to use a gift letter to attempt to defraud the institutional lender.

Whether you find a partner or a generous relative, your ability to cover the cash costs will be the cardinal consideration.

Don't forget that every factor is interrelated: How much cash you'll need will depend on how much you can borrow, which will depend on how much the property is worth and how much you can buy it for, which will depend on how willing the owners are to negotiate, which will depend on how much time is left before the sale and how much you're willing to offer, which will depend on how much cash you'll have to come up with and how much you can finance, etc.

Financing

Beware the "F factor." In real estate finance, this is part of the second half of the monetary equation $C + F + (Co) = T$, where C equals cash needed, as discussed above, F equals the amount to be financed, and T equals the total price of the investment after everything is taken into account (Co is a confusion factor that can be discarded once you understand what's going on).

How much you can borrow, and who you will borrow it from, will be directly affected by how you structure the deal. If there is enough equity available, you may be able to borrow enough to cover the entire purchase price plus all costs. That's exactly what happened to us when we bought the house from the couple in the previous chapter. The bank loaned us $70,000 based on the equity available in the home; which was more than enough to pay all of our costs including paying off the exiting loan and giving the owners some cash for their equity.

Before taking out any loan, weigh the risks involved. Is there enough equity to return a profit greater than your cost of borrowing?

If you have a source of funds you can borrow and if the guaranteed quick-sale return justifies the expense of borrowed money, by all means do so.

When we discuss borrowing, we mean borrowing from a large institutional lender, such as the First National Federal Savings and Loan Thrift Institution of America. If you intend to borrow the money from a private individual, consider taking that person in as a partner instead, as already discussed. You may have to share a greater percentage of the profit, but you are also sharing the risk.

The key word on borrowing is CAUTION. A partnership is often a much safer course to follow.

Working with Bankers

"No man is an island." Or, in modern English, "No person is an island." Either way, the point is valid in any type of real estate investing, and especially in foreclosure investing.

Just to reach this point you may have already worked with law librarians, owners, trustees, Realtors, courthouse personnel, attorneys, and loan officers. You're beginning to assemble quite a team, and a star player will be a good loan officer.

Even if you've found the perfect property—the one loaded with equity that promises a substantial profit—you may have difficulty borrowing money from an institutional lender. If you do, it's only because you don't understand banker mentality. A banker, like an investor, has her own way of looking at things.

A banker (read "loan officer") will lend money based on two factors: risk and return. And since return is written into the contract, risk is everything. Your challenge is to convince your friendly neighborhood loan officer that when you borrow money you will guarantee that it will be returned safe and sound—with interest, of course.

The real secret of getting money out of a lender is understanding the basic Catch-22 paradox of borrowing: bankers are happy to lend you all the money you need—as long as you can prove you don't need it. The funny part is, the individual loan officer is paid to do one thing only: lend money. She wants to lend you the money but she can't unless you can convince her that you can get along fine without it. You must somehow show her that neither she nor the bank is at risk.

When you apply for a real estate loan, risk (and therefore the bank's security) will be broken into two parts: your personal credit rating (and/or the rating of your partner), and the security offered by the equity in the property. To a lesser degree, your personal appearance and demeanor can influence the banker as well. However, it's the impersonal numbers that will carry the most weight.

If you find a million-dollar property that you can buy for $50,000, your personal credit won't matter too much. The banker knows that her bet is covered by the equity in the property. If there is no equity, but you make $100,000 a year and your partners are a Rockefeller and a Kennedy, you can borrow the money based on personal security. But you must have one or the other or a winning combination of the two.

Let's start with the property. By filling out a profitability projection such as the one given in the previous chapter, and by proving that there is a tremendous balance of equity in the property in question, you'll go a long way in convincing a banker to lend you money. By giving her a copy of your projections you'll be giving her something to lock up in her file drawer; something concrete on which she can base—and defend—her judgment.

In the case study outlined in the previous chapter, we knew we could buy the home for under $50,000 and sell it for as much as $120,000. By proving to the banker that there was a potential equity of at least $70,000, we went a long way toward convincing him that he should lend us $70,000 on two days' notice.

That's the power of equity.

Personal credit is the second factor, but it takes a distant second place to a tremendous amount of equity to secure the loan. (And if there isn't a tremendous amount of equity in a transaction, why are you fooling with it?) Nevertheless, your personal balance sheet isn't entirely unimportant. If something does go wrong and the lender is forced to foreclose on your loan, somebody's (read that "the loan officer's") head will roll, especially if the loan was made to a borrower with a poor credit history.

We live in the plastic age where your credit rating is the key to the credit car. Without it you're not going to go anywhere. Whether you invest in real estate or not, you should know how you rate. And finding out is as easy as a trip to the nearest credit reporting agency, which will be listed in the Yellow Pages, not surprisingly, under "Credit Reporting Agencies." For a nominal fee—usually under $10—such an agency will give you a copy of your credit report and explain it in detail.

If your record is clean, you can rest easily, knowing that

your banker will be impressed. If it is dirty, clean it up as much as possible. If there are problems you never knew existed, such as a bill for satin slippers from Siberia that you're sure you never ordered, contact the creditor and have it removed from your record. If the creditor's complaints are valid and they refuse to work with you, you can still deflect some of the heat by adding a 100-word statement that must be included in every credit report.

We don't want to get off on a tangent, but as a side note: If you don't have a credit rating you'll face another Catch-22. It will seem that you can only get credit if you already have credit. And having a solid credit rating, as we've already seen, is important. So how do you establish credit?

One of the easiest ways to get started is to buy a single item, worth under $300, like a microwave, at a major department store, such as J.C. Penney or Sears. Offer to pay half in cash if they will let you charge the other half. If you're holding down a job, they will usually be happy to accept your terms. Make your payments on time until the item is completely paid off, then apply for a few more cards. In no time you'll be up to your neck in plastic.

If you have a poor credit rating, with no cure in sight, chances are you won't get the loan. Better look for a partner with a good credit history while you work on clearing up your tarnished name.

Besides your credit rating, your personal balance sheet is another factor that will influence the banker. If you don't know how to prepare a balance sheet, we suggest that you pick up a book on personal financial management today. Everyone should have a rough idea of his or her net worth, and a banker will certainly want you to complete a balance sheet as part of your application.

The combination of your personal net worth, your credit

rating, and the property's equity must all add up to tip the security scales in your favor, or you won't get the loan. If your application is refused you can always ask the banker where you went wrong, and try again later, or at another bank.

Borrowing from the Owners

As an *ipso-facto* axiom, owners facing foreclosure tend to be short on cash. Therefore the idea of borrowing from the owners appears to be contradiction. On the surface it makes about as much sense as trusting the government. Nevertheless, every owner has one resource you can borrow from: his equity.

Let's say, for the sake of example, that you can buy a particular home for $55,000. The home is worth $80,000, but the owners have agreed to drop the price to $55,000 to avoid the foreclosure sale. There is one lien against it, for $30,000, and you've found a banker willing to lend you $40,000. You seem to be $15,000 short, and you don't have it. You can't find a partner or a wealthy uncle to make up the difference in cash. What can you do?

If the owner isn't pressed for immediate cash, you can borrow his equity from him for a short period of time. In the example, you can use the $40,000 to pay off the first lien, pay closing costs, and give the owner part of his equity. You can then sign a note agreeing to pay the balance within a specific period of time—say three years.

Now you've structured a nothing-down deal in which the banker will lend you part of the money and the seller will lend you the rest. If the home is worth $80,000 you can sell it for $75,000, pay off the original owner's note, and pocket your profit.

While most owners will be in a cash-desperate situation,

there will be a few who, in their eagerness to sell, will take a small amount in cash and the rest on a note. Of course they would prefer all cash, but if a note is the only option that will make the deal work for you, they will have to take it or leave it—and taking it is by far the better option.

Assigning the Contract

There is another technique that doesn't involve cash or financing, which makes it the truest nothing-down strategy of all. You don't have to borrow from a banker, the seller, a partner, or your Mom. It depends on the existence of unique circumstances, but when everything comes together, it means quick profits with very little investment and no ownership of the property whatsoever.

Called *assigning the contract*, it could also be called the "take the money and run" method. It takes only four steps, and can put money—thousands of dollars, in some cases— in your pocket immediately, with no money down.

Step 1: Find a property with substantial ($5,000 or more) instant equity. That means the quick-sale price is at least $5,000 higher than your buying price, and probably $5,000 or more below the actual market value. There must also be some time before the sale, at least a month, and two is better. You can see that this isn't an everyday situation. If the owner has two months to sell, why would she be willing to give up that much equity?

The answer is usually wear and tear on the seller, or distance. If the foreclosure process is in its third or fourth month, some sellers will give up a healthy piece of equity to be rid of a headache. Second, owners who have already abandoned the property and have high-tailed it to other parts are often happy to take what they can salvage from their equity.

It's an unusual situation but it might be wise to hold out for just such a deal the first time you invest.

Step 2: On the purchase offer, in the space reserved for "Buyer," write your name, followed by the words "and/or assigns." For example: *John J. Doe and/or assigns*. By doing this you are reserving the right to assign your interest in the contract to a third party.

Step 3: Set the closing date far enough in the future (at least two months) to give yourself enough time to line up a willing buyer who will pay the full quick-sale price.

Step 4: Sell your interest in the contract to a third party before the closing date. Start making your phone calls immediately—to your entire network of potential partners. Call every Realtor you know, every doctor and lawyer who might be interested, every investor. Explain that you have an instant equity of at least $5,000 that you're willing to sell. Of course, you can sell your position in the contract for as much or as little as the market will bear, and investors can more than double their money when they sell the property.

It's a marvelous way to make money; you can get out of the deal cash-free and deposit your earnings in Hip-Pocket National Bank without ever owning the property. It's like having your cake and eating it too—and sharing a slice with someone else while you're at it.

The only cash involved for you will be the earnest money deposit required when you make your offer. Don't think in terms of thousands or even hundreds of dollars. That deposit is a show of good faith, and in most real estate transactions it should be high enough to make the sellers feel secure during the escrow period. However, when there is an impending foreclosure and only a short time left for reinstatement, the escrow period may be as short as two weeks. Offering $20 to $100 isn't out of line. If the sellers object, explain that a larger deposit is unnecessary due to the extremely short escrow period.

Your title officer or real estate attorney can help you with the particulars. Actually, assigning a contract is a very simple process, and once you've done it successfully you'll be able to repeat the process as often as you can find properties that fit the profile.

Putting It All Together

The money factor, including the amount to be financed and the cash expenses, is a complex subject to cover in a few pages. Even real estate professionals, with years of experience, take their time when treading on this ground. It will take practical experience before you will feel comfortable structuring a deal, and we heartily recommend that you read other books on the subject of real estate finance.

Before we move on to the other factors that affect your strategic planning—time and the owner—let's take a couple of examples and attempt to structure financial arrangements that will allow us to buy the properties.

Example I

You're planning to buy a home valued at $85,000, with a quick-sale value of $75,000. The owner is willing to sell for only $55,000, but insists on getting his equity in cash. The foreclosure auction is three weeks away.

There is only one lien in existence, with a balance of $35,000. Delinquent payments and legal fees have piled up to a total cost of $2,500, which the owner expects you to pay.

Closing costs will be another $2,500. You've found a banker willing to lend you $50,000, based on your good credit and the equity in the home.

Let's say further that you only have $1,000 of your own

money available for investing. What is your total out-of-pocket expense, how much will you have to finance, and where will you get the money?

Before answering let's list all of the factors:

Value of property	$ 85,000
Purchase price	55,000
Quick-sale value	75,000
Lien	35,000
Delinquent payments	2,500
Closing costs	2,500
Money you can borrow	50,000
Money available for investing	1,000

The problem is partly solved already, because you know that the most you can borrow from a conventional lender is $50,000, and you also know that the owner is unwilling to let you borrow his equity.

We want you to solve this one on your own before you look at the answers listed below. Keep in mind that there is no single best answer. Every situation may have dozens of possible solutions. Work out what you consider to be a workable answer before you read the suggestions.

Solution 1: Take on a Partner

This one seems the easiest. The owner insists on getting $55,000, with which he will pay off the $35,000 lien, keeping the remainder. Your additional expenses, including back payments and closing costs, are another $5,000, for a total of $60,000. You can borrow only $50,000, leaving a balance of $10,000. Your $1,000 personal investment reduces the amount you still need to $9,000.

Find a partner who is willing to put up $9,000 in exchange

for a share of the profit. You can easily sell the property for $75,000, making $15,000 profit. Split the profit with your partner; you will each make $7,500 on the money invested. True, your return on investment is much greater than your partner's, but then you're the one who did most of the work right?

Solution 2: Negotiate
The owner *said* he wouldn't take less than $55,000, and he *said* he wanted his equity in cash, but the sale isn't final until the contract is signed. With three weeks left until the auction, time is on your side. We'll cover negotiating at the end of this chapter and you'll see that you're always in the driver's seat.

Solution 3: Don't Buy
Better safe than sorry, as mom used to say. Even if everything falls into line, the most you can make is $15,000, which could get eaten up in carrying costs, Realtor's commissions, and other hidden expenses. It *looks* like a good deal, but if you can't find a partner and if the owner won't negotiate, it might be better to chalk this one up to learning experience and move on.

Example II
Another house, market value of $122,000. You think it would sell within two months for $100,000 (or in one month for $95,000), and the auction is four weeks away. There is one lien against the property, a first mortgage, for $52,000. All delinquent payments and legal fees total $4,000, and if you agree to cover all cash expenses, the owner is willing to work out a part-cash, part- financed deal. (She's flexible on how much equity she needs, but she absolutely must have $10,000 cash to get into a condo.) You'll have to pay all

closing costs, totalling $5,000.

The owner is sick of opening threatening letters and wants out as soon as possible.

You've lined up a $55,000 loan with a local mortgage lender, and you have $5,000 cash that you could invest. You also have a partner who has invested with you in the past that you're sure could scrape up $10,000 or more.

Confused? This might help:

Market value	$122,000
Purchase price	negotiable
Quick-sale price (2 mos.)	100,000
Quick-sale price (1 mo.)	95,000
Lien	52,000
Delinquent payments and legal fees	4,000
Closing costs	5,000
Seller's need	10,000 cash
Money you can borrow	55,000
Money available for investing	5,000
Partner's contribution	10,000 +

Any clearer? Let's begin the problem-solving process by determining exactly how much you will pay for the property. You know the seller is flexible, and, while she doesn't have to sell right away, she is more than ready to work with you on terms.

Let's assume that you agree to pay her $10,000 cash, and you will also pay all closing costs, back payments, and legal fees. Also, you will cure the outstanding balance of $52,000 on her first mortgage.

The minimum you will have to come up with, in cash and financing, is $71,000 ($52,000 + $10,000 + $4,000 + $5,000).

Solution 1: Assign the Contract

Tie this one down with a contract and sell the contract quickly, before the auction. You could agree to her terms, offering to pay her $10,000 cash, pay all delinquent charges and closing costs. She would get what she needs, if not what she wants, and you could assign the contract to another investor for, say, $79,000.

Your profit would be about $8,000 cash; the investor could pay $79,000 for a home worth at least $100,000; and you would be out of the picture with cash in your pocket—never having owned the property a day in your life!

Solution 2: Buy/Sell

Solution one may work, but it depends on finding another investor willing to work with you. There is a safer bet: buying and selling the property yourself.

The numbers in this case aren't very far away from our actual case study of the previous chapter. You could make the same offer we did: you will borrow as much as the bank will allow you to borrow, and then you will pay off all existing debts, pay all closing costs, and split the remainder.

In this case you may be able to borrow the entire $71,000 you need to buy the property. That would put you into the deal with absolutely no money out of your own wallet.

The problem is, once you've paid all debts and closing costs you will only have $10,000. And if you split it, the owner won't get her $10,000 cash. There are two possible solutions to that problem: First, you can give her the $10,000. You will own a home worth over $100,000, and you will have purchased it for only $71,000—all borrowed money!

Second, you can negotiate with the owner, agreeing to give her $5,000 now and half the profit from the sale. If you

110

can sell for $100,000 you can pay two months' carrying costs, Realtor's commissions (if you sell through an agent), and closing costs, and you'll probably still clear $15,000 to $20,000 profit. The owner will be better off accepting this deal if she can afford to wait a couple of months.

TIME

Time is the second factor that will affect your plan. Time considerations include more than how many days are left before the auction. How you'll structure your offer will depend on how long you plan to own the property once you've bought it; how long it will take to sell at any given price; how much time pressure there is on the owner to sell to you.

How vital time is to your strategy becomes apparent when you make an offer to an owner who has missed two payments, and then make the same offer six months later, when the auction is a week away. If there are three months left before the trustee's sale, it might be a good idea to try assigning the contract. If there is only one week left, it probably won't work.

We have found a good system that takes advantage of time every time, time after time. We make the first offer long before the actual sale date, and we make it a competitive offer. However, we put no pressure on the owners. They can turn down the offer and we won't mind at all. If they accept it, we have a contract we can assign. If they reject it, we wait.

Months later, as the sale date approaches, we make a second offer. We have more at risk, and the owners have more to lose, so our offer will likely be for less. We always structure an offer that allows the owners to walk away with at least a few thousand dollars, and again we don't attempt to pressure them into accepting.

If the owners haven't taken advantage of the many opportunities to sell during the last month before the auction, we'll make a last attempt. The pressure is on both parties to put together a deal, so we are usually able to come to an agreement; however, very few properties that have a lot of equity available make it this far.

At every step along the timeline the owners can find a buyer and get rid of their headache. If they choose not to sell until the last few hours, it isn't your fault. And, as we've stressed before, they are much, much better off having you buy the property than letting it go to auction.

The second time factor is the length of time you plan to own the property, and the effect of that time period on your projected profit. For example, if you will be buying a house for $75,000, with monthly payments of $750, four months of ownership will cost a minimum of $3,000.

You must decide how long you will own the property, versus how much you can sell it for. The accompanying graph demonstrates the relationship between time for sale and selling price.

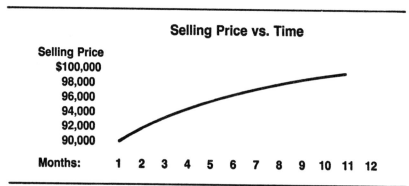

As you can see, the property in this example will sell in less than a month at $90,000 (what you might call its extremely-quick-sale value). At $92,000 it will take about two months; at $94,000, four months. And so on, until, at $100,000 it will take over a year.

The mythical "market value" is the price it will sell for within four to six months—about $95,000. The quick-sale value that we've used throughout this book is at the two-to three-month mark, perhaps $93,000.

If we are using this example, which you purchased for $75,000, your return each month, after paying, say, $950 a month in monthly mortgage payments and maintenance, is as follows (excluding selling costs):

Selling Price Over Time

Time	Selling Price	Total Costs	Profit
1 mo.	$ 90,000	$ 75,950	$ 14,050
2 mos.	$ 92,000	$ 76,900	$ 15,100
3 mos.	$ 93,100	$ 77,850	$ 15,250
4 mos.	$ 94,000	$ 78,800	$ 15,200
5 mos.	$ 94,800	$ 79,750	$ 15,050
6 mos.	$ 95,450	$ 80,700	$ 14,750
7 mos.	$ 96,000	$ 81,650	$ 14,350
8 mos.	$ 96,500	$ 82,600	$ 13,900
9 mos.	$ 96,975	$ 83,550	$ 13,425
10 mos.	$ 97,425	$ 84,500	$ 12,925
11 mos.	$ 97,850	$ 85,450	$ 12,400
12 mos.	$ 98,200	$ 86,400	$ 11,800

Let's plug the results into a time graph for a clearer picture of how the length of time you own a property affects your profit.

Every investment will have its own unique curve, depending on how quickly property is appreciating in a given area; how high the monthly carrying costs will be; and a host of other factors that will vary from one deal to the next.

The profit/time curve will tell you how long you should hold onto a piece of real estate before selling it, for maximum profitability. In the example just used, it's apparent that the

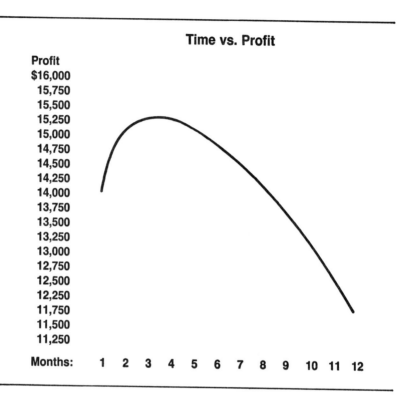

Time vs. Profit

Profit
$16,000
15,750
15,500
15,250
15,000
14,750
14,500
14,250
14,000
13,750
13,500
13,250
13,000
12,750
12,500
12,250
11,750
11,500
11,250

Months: 1 2 3 4 5 6 7 8 9 10 11 12

maximum profit is to be made by selling in the third month of ownership.

Unfortunately, predicting the best part of the curve is a near impossibility. It will always be an educated guess. Fortunately, you can educate yourself, over a period of time, so you can approximate the peak of the curve and make your investing decision accordingly.

In the case above, you've determined that you will hold the property for three months and sell it for $93,100. That will be an important factor when you make your offer.

Time, for both the owner and the investor, can be an enemy or a friend. To invest effectively you must stay in control. Take time into account, but never allow it to get the best of you.

THE OWNERS

The final factor consists of the owners. Some will be antagonistic and embittered; others will be friendly and grateful. Most will be confused, frightened, suspicious. Some will jump at any offer. Others will hold out until the last day, waiting for someone to give them full value for their equity.

Negotiating

When you talk to an owner for the first time, approach with caution. A desperate owner can be like a cornered animal: unpredictable, sometimes even vicious. That isn't meant as an insult. Put yourself in the same position. This is the house your first child was born in; the indoor jacuzzi that occasionally works was your first home-improvement project. The carpet on the stairs is worn, but it was worn down by the pitter-patter of tiny feet running down to open Christmas presents. Now, just because you were laid off and haven't been able to keep up the payments for two months, you've received a notice of default. You're scared. You're frustrated. The phone rings. You pick it up.

"Hi, I'm Joe Investor, foreclosure specialist, and I hear you're going to be foreclosed on . . ."

It just won't work. As an investor—a foreclosure specialist—you need empathy, not just sympathy. The owners have a real problem that just won't go away, and you have a solution. Your first step is to establish rapport and prove to them that you're calling on them to help. Don't be afraid of their reaction; you may be the first one to approach them without an overdue bill in your hand.

If you have prepared yourself, you will already know exactly how far behind the owners have fallen in their payments. You'll know the market value of the house. You should have a good idea what kind of offer you'd like to present. However, you shouldn't approach the owners with a know-it-all attitude. If you start spouting off facts and figures, such as "You are two months behind on your mortgage payments of $445.23," they will feel violated. To them, that is highly personal information.

Instead, approach them as a sincere professional who can help them out of a tough situation. A touch of sympathy isn't out of line, although gushing pity is as likely to be as offensive as outright cruelty. There are a few definite do's and don'ts when talking face to face with owners, about their situation:

DO's

□ Do knock on the door with confidence.

□ Do smile.

□ Do explain that you're there to help.

□ Do be unabrasive and understanding.

□ Do empathize. Try to put yourself in the owners' shoes.

□ Do mention that the lender *will* foreclose, and that selling is a better option than allowing that to happen.

□ Do explain that foreclosure will continue to show on a credit report for seven years. It already will show a late payment, but that is nothing compared to a foreclosure.

DON'Ts

□ Don't threaten the owners.

□ Don't tell them they will be thrown out into the street.

□ Don't offer them money and tell them to get out.

□ Don't present yourself as a shark at a feeding frenzy.

□ Don't present yourself as a first-time investor.

□ Don't force the issue. If they aren't ready to sell, leave them an offer for their consideration, along with your business card.

□ Don't promise to reinstate their loan if you can't. For that matter, don't make any promises you can't keep.

□ Don't underdress or overdress. Something clean and casual will work best. Also, don't drive up in a brand new Mercedes or an ancient Chevy. If you overdo it, you'll be seen as a slick investor. If you underdo it, your credibility will be questioned.

Your natural inclination may be to assume that everyone you talk to knows at least as much as—and probably more than—you do about foreclosures. That isn't true; just from the reading you've already done you know more about the foreclosure process than most Realtors! Very few homeowners have more than the foggiest notion of what is involved in a foreclosure. Their notice of default never mentioned a 90-day reinstatement period. It seems to call the entire loan due and payable.

Ask if you can sit down with the owners and discuss their options with them. They may be very relieved to hear a friendly, knowledgable voice. Carefully explain the alternatives they are facing: They can reinstate their loan *if* they can make up all of their back payments within the 90-day period. They can wait for the foreclosure sale and get evicted. They can desert the property. Or they can sell it now. If they can beg, borrow or steal the money in time (don't suggest the third alternative), you wish them well. If they can't, they must sell soon to protect their credit rating. You are offering them that opportunity. You can *stop* the foreclosure process.

An important point here: You won't be convincing if you're not convinced. You are saving them from a horrible experience. True, you are doing it to make money, but you are saving them from embarrassment, further hassles, and a giant black mark on their credit rating. Once you understand that, you can help owners see it as well.

Every foreclosure situation is unique, so there is no set rule for negotiating. Here are a few common causes of foreclosure:

□ Death of a spouse.
□ Illness and out of work.
□ Hospitalization and out of work.
□ Loss of a job.
□ Stock market losses.
□ Real estate investment losses.
□ Divorce.
□ Separation.
□ Seasonal employment.
□ Too much debt.
□ Business failure.
□ Gambling debts.
□ Other unexpected expenses

The reasons are practically endless. Each requires a different approach. You will often be dealing with people who feel they are failures. And most of them are thinking something like:

"The lender won't really foreclose."
"I will be able to work with the lender."
"I will borrow the money to reinstate the loan."
"I will save the money I need before foreclosure."
"I can always sell the house and pay the lender."
"I can always get a second job."
"I can always sell the car."
"I can always sell the boat."
"I can always sell the camper."

"I can always sell another piece of property."
"I can always win the big jackpot in Vegas."
"I can always . . . ."

Convincing the owners to sell won't be easy. In fact, it will sometimes be impossible. Some owners will watch their home sold at auction before they'll sell, and there is nothing you can do about it.

Find out the owner's needs, not wants. That is standard negotiating practice. Of course they want someone to pay them cash for every penny, but they need someone to get them out of the mess they're in and give them thousands of dollars of walking money.

If you can't meet their cash needs, you can offer something more creative, such as:

□ Trade another property with a smaller equity.
□ Shared equity.
□ Trade bond for equity.
□ Trade car for equity.
□ Offer them future money. For example, balloon notes due in 5, 10, and 15 years.
□ Offer relocation expense for equity.
□ Free rent for equity.
□ Any combination of financing, cash and assets.

Don't restrict yourself to thinking in terms of strictly cash, and be sure to release skeptical sellers from the same restriction. The fact is that unless someone rescues them soon, they will lose all of their equity. With that realization often comes a softening of their resolve.

Show them the alternatives they face without pressuring them. If they show disbelief, invite them to discuss it with any attorney. All you need to do when you first approach an owner is to open up a door and let in a little light they may not have seen before. Give them hope.

A frequently asked question is, "Why wouldn't an owner simply sell his property on the open market, rather than accepting my terms?" Three reasons: lack of knowledge, lack of time, and stress. Few homeowners consider themselves investors. Often, all they know about home buying is what they learned when a real estate agent sold them their own home—and the agent did all the paperwork. Now, facing foreclosure, they may not even think of selling. Or, if they have considered it, they may not know where to begin. Some owners will list their houses with an agent, or try to sell it themselves but they run into the second problem—lack of time.

Remember, the notice of default may give the owners the impression that the entire loan balance is immediately due. They already knew they were in default, but when they receive the dreaded NOD they realize that time is running short.

The combined factors of ignorance and lack of time can cause severe stress on owners. They may be frantically trying to figure out how to sell their burden in the limited time available, when you show up at the door with an offer. If you approach with the right combination of knowledge and sincere understanding, you might be surprised to find a red carpet rolled out at your arrival.

Sometimes a property is in foreclosure because it has been on the market for a few months. An owner, realizing that he can no longer afford his payment, may list a house and default on his loan at the same time. If the house doesn't sell within the listing period, it will be a candidate for foreclosure. He has become disillusioned with his own efforts and is ready to throw in the towel. He needs your help.

Another common question is, "Why doesn't the owner file bankruptcy to gain time to sell, rather than lose his equity and sell to me?" A fair question, but it misses the point: Bankruptcy only delays the foreclosure; it rarely solves the problem. It might buy the owner an extra six months, but that generally won't be enough time for an inexperienced seller. Also, very few people are willing to expose themselves to the public embarrassment of bankruptcy.

YOUR INVESTMENT PLAN

Barring unforseen complications, such as hidden liens or hidden property damages, you've gathered enough information to plan your investment strategy. You know how much you can offer and you know about how much the owners will accept. You know approximately how much profit is available, depending on how much you can sell it for within any given selling period. You know how much cash you can raise and how much you can finance.

Like snowflakes and fingerprints, no two investments will be alike. It becomes therefore increasingly difficult for any book such as this one to hold your hand and tell you exactly what to do. The forms you've filled out, combined with your research, will help you decide how much to offer, and on what terms you'll make your offer. Will you give the owners half your profit when you sell, in exchange for a nothing-down deal? Will you borrow the entire purchase price from the bank?

If the idea of planning your first offer is either confusing or unnerving, you haven't yet been in the actual situation. You'll find that once you've done all the homework we've assigned, there will only be a few good options, and you won't have any difficulty coming up with two or three workable plans.

The time has come to do more than think and plan. In the next chapter we'll go through the mechanics of making an actual offer and getting it accepted.

CHAPTER FIVE

Buying Before The Sale: Making The Offer & Closing The Deal

It's not too late to back out! You haven't actually committed yourself on paper, all you've done is talk about buying the property. You can walk away older, wiser, and no richer.

If you're determined to forge ahead, the rest of your wheeling and dealing will take place in three stages: making the written offer, the escrow period, and the closing.

THE OFFER

Writing and presenting your first offer may be a heart-thumping experience. It's the concrete step that separates the would-be investors from the real ones. And it's not a step to be taken lightly.

Your offer will include the price and the terms of the purchase. Therefore, you must be willing to tie yourself to the terms of the contract.

If you've shopped at all for financing, you will by now know approximately how much you can borrow. You will also know how much cash you'll need (your own cash or a partner's), based on how much you plan to offer. However, before you actually present a written offer, you should do one more thing: appraise the property's value to the nearest dollar.

Additionally, you should continue to negotiate with the owner, without actually committing yourself to any specific offer. The negotiations will be an ongoing process right up until the offer is signed and countersigned. In some cases that may mean 10 face-to-face meetings, but you will gain ground in every meeting.

Appraisal

Your quick, glossy market appraisal, in which you determined the rough market value (as well as the quick-sale price) of the property, was only a beginning. Before agreeing to purchase any piece of real estate, you'd better take the time to inspect and appraise the property.

Appraisal is a two-part game. In the first half you will find out what other similar properties are selling for. In the second you will inspect the subject property for individual quirks that will make it more or less valuable.

Both halves can be done by professionals, and it wouldn't hurt to employ their services, especially for your first few investments. A professional appraiser, found in the Yellow Pages under "Appraisers" or "Real Estate Appraisers," will charge a reasonable fee ("reasonable" varies from one locale to another, so compare prices) to determine the market value of any property.

In appraising residential real estate, the appraiser will employ a method called *market comparison*. He will find at least three other similar properties in similar locations that have sold within the last three months. Taking the selling price of each comparison property, he will make adjustments based on differences between that property and the subject property, and then average the three adjusted values to arrive at a best-guess appraisal.

For example, if the house under consideration has a fireplace, but the first comparable property does not, the appraiser would add the value of a fireplace to the selling price of the comparable house to adjust its market value. If your subject house has two bathrooms and the second comparable house has three, the appraiser will subtract the value of a bathroom from the selling price of comparable two. The average of the three comparable properties, after adjustments for differences, will give you a good idea of the actual market value of your proposed purchase.

Many investors with a few deals under their belts will bypass the professional appraisal, saving themselves up to $200. For a beginning investor, however, the money is usually well spent.

If you do pay for an appraisal, we have two more suggestions: First, ask the appraiser before you hire him if you can tag along and learn the tricks of the trade. If the answer is no, keep looking until you get a yes. The education will be worth much more than the fee, even if you don't buy the property.

Second, if you're confident that you've pinpointed the market value of the property within a thousand dollars, you can tie the property up with a contract before you have the property appraised. In a few pages we'll be giving you several clauses to insert into your contract to protect yourself, and one of them involves building an escape hatch that will allow you to excuse yourself from the contract if the appraised value of the house is lower than your purchase price.

There is no law that says you must have real estate professionally appraised. You can perform your own market comparison and you will no doubt want to do exactly that after you've closed a few deals. Also, if there are no structural defects, and if there is enough instant equity available, you don't have to know the value of a property to the nearest dollar to make money. If similar properties are selling for $65,000, and you can buy the house for $45,000, does it matter that its exact market value (if there is such a thing) is $46,250?

Inspection

Inspecting a house is, of course, part of the appraisal, but at the same time it is a different subject. A professional inspector can be called in to look closely for hidden defects, and we recommend that you use an inspector on every deal.

We should say "inspections," rather than "inspection." You will probably inspect every property at least four times: once when you first see it; once again, more closely, before making an offer; once with the help of a professional; and then again one day before the closing.

The first inspection, a "curbside" inspection, begins the minute you drive down the street toward the property. It includes your general feeling about the area. Is it a peaceful, polite looking suburb, or is it a hotbed of drug-maddened motorcycle gangs? As you pull up to the curb, are you struck by the neatness of the shrubbery, or the trash piled up around the garage door? Curb appeal is the first step in property inspection and appraisal. If the neighboring houses are a mess, no amount of clean-up on your part will make the house more salable.

As you walk across the grass toward the front door, is it the clean lines of the trim paint that catch your eye, or the screen door hanging askew? When the owner takes you through her home for the first time, what is your general impression? Are there large cracks running up the walls? Are the appliances 50 years old? Is the tub rust-stained?

Welcome to property inspection, the fine art of finding fault. As you walk through, look at the house through the eyes of the person you will be selling to. That person (or couple) won't be an investor. It will be a person who wants a home. And who wants a new home with rust stains in the tub?

The first inspection will often make or break a deal. If there are enough faults to put you on your guard, you will have to adjust your estimated market value accordingly. Every home on the block might be selling for $65,000, but if there are defects in the house that you can't correct, you may have difficulty selling for $50,000.

Those faults are often great negotiating points. With a few well placed "Mmmmmmms" and one or two "Harrmphs," accompanied by polite but pointed questions, such as, "The tub has a slight leak in it, doesn't it?" you may negotiate several thousand dollars off the price.

If you haven't been driven away from the deal by the minor problems, and you and the seller are into serious negotiations, the second inspection should be done room by room. Show up at an appointed hour, dressed for inspecting work. Look suitably serious, and equip yourself with the following:

□ A notebook.

□ A pair of sturdy work gloves.

□ A small pocket knife.

□ A level.

□ A hammer for tapping walls and floors (it convinces sellers that you really know what you're doing).

□ A tape measure (the longer the better).

□ A flashlight.

□ A screwdriver.

The Exterior

Start with the outside and work your way inward. Look at

the landscaping: the trees, shrubbery, lawn. Is it dead or alive? Does it add any value to the property? If it's dying, how much work will be required to bring it back to life? Large, dead trees will have to be uprooted and hauled away, an expensive chore.

Look at the cement work. Are there large cracks in the driveway? If there are retaining walls, what condition are they in? Cracks in the walls, sidewalks, or the driveway indicate that the earth has settled. A few cracks are to be expected, but major rifts may indicate serious problems. Look at surrounding properties and the street itself. If an entire neighborhood is plagued by cracks, you may be buying into a very unstable area.

Drainage is another vital factor. Does the property slope away from the house? If there is a heavy storm, which way will the water run? If you miss this one element, it may prove costly three months later, when you try to sell during the rainy season.

Check the garage next. You will need your level and your flashlight here, as you check out the walls and the roof. Shine the light on the ceiling. Are there any stains, especially where the walls meet the ceiling? Ask the owner about any marks: "Looks like you've had a little problem there with leaks, right?"

Use the level to verify that the walls are vertical and the window and door frames are in line. Is the header above the garage door level? Note any defects in your pad, accompanied by tactful criticisms that allow the owner to apologetically explain their existence.

Look at the roof of the entire home, from every side. Are the shingles even? Are there bald spots? Are there noticeable dips or bulges? If the roofing material is discolored, especially in one spot, there may be water damage.

Also on the outside of the house, look for amenities. Are there electrical outlets all around? If not, is there at least one outlet on the patio? How many hose connections are there? Even a small house should have one tap at the front and one at the back.

Check out the foundation with your penknife. Stab the mortar. Is it solid or soft? Loose or crumbling mortar is a danger signal. Check the window sills in the same way. The wood and caulking should be firm, not pulpy.

The foundation wall should stick up out of the ground several inches all the way around the house. At no point should the wood of the frame come in contact with the ground. Look for small tubes of mud leading from the ground to the frame. These innocent-looking shafts are termite tunnels, and you don't want your potential investment used as a main course.

The Interior

Start at the bottom and work your way up. In California and other coastal states that will mean the crawl space. In the rest of the country it means the basement.

The crawlspace is a nitty gritty, well-named place. With flashlight in hand, inspect the woodwork and the interior of the foundation. Splotchy, measle-looking woodwork may indicate water damage. Vertical cracks in the cement mean settling. There will always be some natural settling of the ground, so a few small cracks in an older home are to be expected. In fact, if a house has stood for a dozen years or more and has only a few cracks to show for it, it's in good shape, settlement-wise. In a new home, however, cracks may mean the beginning of serious problems and probably should be avoided.

In a finished basement you won't be able to see the foundation; however, you can inspect the walls, especially around the window wells, for water damage. On a cement floor, tap with your hammer. A flat, dull sound indicates a thick, solid floor. A hollow or high-pitched echo may mean thin material or a hollow space below the cement, both of which are danger signals that should be noted.

On every floor you can check the walls and door frames for evenness. Sighting along any wall you can tell whether or not they line up, and with your level you can determine whether or not the house is standing straight.

Use your tape measure throughout to measure the dimensions of each room. Draw a rough floor plan, including dimensions, that you can use later to analyze traffic flow and comfort. A room can seem twice as large empty as it will when filled with furniture.

Inspect the electrical outlets throughout. Are there enough outlets in every room? It's a good idea to have at least one every six feet or so in most rooms, and in the kitchen there should be enough to support the host of appliances that most Americans couldn't live without, from the food processor to the microwave.

Another kitchen consideration is lighting. A kitchen should have a sunny, airy, friendly feeling. Is there enough light? Is there a window above the sink? Does it have a cheery, early-morning feeling, or do you feel like you're cooking in a dungeon? The kitchen is the first selling point in a house, followed by the bathrooms. Both should be clean, well-lit, and homey.

Open the cupboards beneath every sink. Are there signs of water damage? Are the pipes rusty? Turn on every faucet in the house but not at the same time. Is there enough water pressure? Turn on the hot water in the kitchen. How long does it take for it to get warm? Do any of the faucets leak around the handle? Do they shut off completely when turned off?

In the bathrooms, flush every toilet and inspect around their bases for cracked or bulging linoleum. (As a side note, you can often tell the age of a property by taking the lid off the toilet. The date of manufacture will be stamped inside the tank, and the toilet is one fixture that is installed when the house is built.)

The reason for paying so much attention to the plumbing and electrical aspects of the house is that these repairs are often the most costly. It pays to take notice of such problems before you buy. Once the property is yours, so is the expense of calling in Mr. Plumber.

In the attic, inspect for insulation and, of course, water damage. Insulation in the attic is vital in both cold and hot climates—20% to 30% of all heat loss and heat gain takes place in the attic, and proper insulation is the only shield against mother nature's influence. You can check the insulation in the exterior walls throughout the house by removing the plastic plate the surrounds the electrical outlets. With your screwdriver (and you thought you weren't going to use it), gently poke through the wall to the exterior side. If you meet spongy resistance, you've found insulation—that's good. If, throughout the house, you hit the outside wall without meeting resistance, the walls probably aren't insulated. Harrumph a little and make a note of it.

There are other important considerations. How large is the water heater? How old is the heating and air conditioning system? Try out both systems no matter what time of year it is. A broken heater may go unnoticed in July, but try selling the house in December!

Make a note of all amenities. Is there a dishwasher? A trash compactor? A fireplace? Any other extras? Which are to be included in the sale and which will go with the sellers? Make a list of all needed repairs that you've spotted, along with estimated costs for improvements. You can make your notes in full view of the sellers, added ammunition when the time comes to strike a bargain.

Your inspection can be as cursory or as involved as you want to make it. To make the chore easier, use the accompanying checklist:

Inspection Checklist

Neighborhood condition: _____

Exterior condition: _____

Yard

    landscape _____

    slope _____

    drainage _____

    structure _____

    termites _____

    electrical _____

    hose connections _____

    cement condition _____

Garage

    level _____

    windows and door frames _____

    water damage _____

    cracks in wall or floors _____

Roof

    condition of roofing material _____

    slope _____

    bald patches _____

    missing shingles _____

    water damage _____

Basement or crawlspace

    cracks _____

    water damage _____

    signs of termites _____

    solid floor _____

    level _____

Interior

Electrical outlets

    condition _____

    are there enough? _____

Kitchen
  well lit; airy ——————————————
  water pressure OK, no leaks ——————————
  hot water adequate ——————————————
  window above sink ——————————————
  clean, bright, friendly ————————————
  outlets adequate ——————————————
Bathrooms
  clean tubs, toilets, sinks ————————————
  well lit ——————————————
Plumbing
  hot water throughout ————————————
  water pressure ——————————————
  leaks under sinks ——————————————
  water damage throughout ——————————
Heating
  age of system ——————————————
  type of system—steam, gas, oil ——————————
  functioning ——————————————
Attic
  insulation ——————————————
  water damage ——————————————

When you've completed your inspection, adjust your estimate of value accordingly. If you're not sure how much adjustment is needed, guess high. If you're completely out of your league, call in an expert.

There is much more inspecting that can—and probably should—be done, preferably by a professional. If you've done this much, you're at least in a position of strength as you continue your negotiations. If you've encountered no serious structural, electrical, or plumbing damages, you will be ready to enter the last leg of the negotiating process.

You can do a more thorough inspecting job yourself, of course, and you should if you don't want to pay a professional inspector. In that case, we recommend "How to Inspect a House," by George Hoffman (Addison Wesley, 1985).

Thanks to another clause we'll be giving you shortly, you can make your offer now and have the inspection done later.

If the inspection report uncovers hidden defects you can back out of the deal without losing anything more than the inspection fee.

WORKING OUT THE DETAILS

You should be getting to know the owners quite well at this point, a fact that may work in your favor—and then again may work against you. Depending on your personality, your heart may be getting tangled up in the deal. You must keep your purpose in mind, and in perspective.

In the last chapter we talked about your opening gambits as you began the negotiation process with the owners. Now that you have a closer look, and have designed a tentative business plan, your face-to-face dealings will continue to be increasingly focused and your skills as a buyer will be tested.

As the moment draws ever nearer when you will present your official written offer, your negotiations with the owners will get more intense. Every deal will have its own parameters and therefore its own outcome, but we can give you several negotiating pointers:

Time is on your side.

Time pressure has already been mentioned. As the foreclosure approaches, the owners' need to sell increases. Your need to buy, however, should remain constant. Even if you lose the deal you will actually lose nothing but some time and a few expenses.

Concentrate on the sellers' needs.

Sellers always want their entire equity—preferably in cash. However, needs and wants are two very different animals. Gus wanted us to give him $120,000 for his home, but he needed to sell it for whatever he could get before the auction.

134

Find out the sellers' needs. Do they absolutely have to have $10,000 cash up front? Why do they need that much money? If they won't tell you why, or if they want to know what difference it makes, explain that it's your money, and you want to know what your money will be used for. Tell them that you will do everything you can to get the money, but you may not be able to meet their demands.

Even the sellers may not recognize their true needs until shortly before the sale. Don't allow their wants to rule the negotiations.

Keep the negotiations oral until the last moment.
There is as much difference between oral negotiations and a written offer as there is between a dog and a bowling ball. Keep everything open to change until you're ready to make a commitment. If you're not satisfied with the verbal negotiations, allow time to take its toll, and add a bit of pressure by saying, "It's too bad we can't come to terms after all the work we've done together."

Don't fall in love with the property or the owners.
Business is business, and if you're not in business, you have no business investing in real estate. While we advocate fairness, we do so with the strong warning to avoid losing sight of your investing goals. Until you've made your first million, leave philanthropy to retired movie actors.

Once you fall in love with the property or the owners, to the point where you're willing to sacrifice a good deal, you should turn your back on the transaction and head for the hills.

Be courteous and considerate, but candid.
If you have discovered problems during your inspection,

point them out. Be honest with the owners about your objections, without being offensive. If you can only pay the owners a couple thousand dollars for their equity, be honest about it and explain why you are restricted from giving them as much as they think they need.

If the best you can do is a thousand now and another thousand when you sell, say so. They can turn down your offer, but they should be aware that the alternative is an auction in which they will receive nothing whatsoever.

Give and take.

If they won't give on the price, they may give on terms. If they won't include all of the appliances, they may give in on price. If they absolutely must have $10,000 cash, they may give up the appliances and they may not care at all about price.

In other words, there must be give and take in any negotiation. If you don't have enough cash to meet their needs, offer something in place of cash, or ask for a lower selling price so you can arrange for easier financing. Every time negotiations seem to be breaking down, fix them with a compromise.

Leave yourself some space.

If the property is worth $70,000, don't start bidding at $65,000 and expect to get a good deal. A better starting point, especially in a foreclosure situation, is perhaps as low as $30,000. The owner may be outraged, but it makes your next bid of $35,000 seem much better by comparison.

If the seller owes $35,000, including back payments, then $40,000 wouldn't be a bad starting place, and if you ended up at $45,000 or $50,000, you would both be getting a great deal. The seller would certainly rather have $10,000 or $15,000 than nothing, and you could clear the same amount—or more—when you sold the property. However, if you begin the bidding at $50,000, there's no way you're going to buy it for less than $55,000 or $60,000.

PREPARING THE WRITTEN OFFER

The last stage before the actual written offer is a sit-down talk with the sellers. You should have a crystal-clear understanding of each other's positions, even if you haven't reached a verbal agreement.

To bring you current, we'll use another example:

You've found a property in foreclosure, with a month left before the sale. Its market value is about $85,000, quick-sale value between $75,000 and $80,000. Including the loan balance, back payments and other assorted fees, the owner needs $48,000 cash just to walk away empty-handed.

With your handy analysis sheets you've determined that you can pay all costs for buying, fixing, and selling the property and still clear $18,000 profit within three months. This is a multiple choice question: How much will you offer the seller, and on what terms?

a) You will buy the property for $52,000, giving the owner $2,000 cash for his equity now, and another $2,000 in three months.

b) You offer $52,000, giving him no money down now (you'll need all the cash to cover closing costs) and $5,000 in three months.

c) You offer $60,000, giving the owner $1,000 now, $1,000 in one month, and $10,000 in six months.

d) There isn't enough information in the example to make a decision.

e) Six ducks and a pig at closing, the balance to be paid at the end of the summer in horses and cows, with interest in the form of wheat and corn.

The correct answer is any of the above, and anything else you may have come up with on your own. As long as you've done enough market research to assure yourself that you're getting a good deal, you can structure any offer that you think will be accepted.

In the example above you know for a fact that the owner's minimum need is for someone to solve his $48,000 problem. In addition, you know that he needs some incentive for working with you, whether it's six pigs a year from now or $10,000 cash.

In reality, by the time you reach this stage you'll have an unambiguous understanding of what the owner needs and therefore what kind of offer will fly. Your written offer must at least satisfy those needs.

In our example we could offer anything from $48,000 up to—well, up to as much as we were willing to offer. After several days—and possibly weeks—of haggling, we know the owner will accept, say, an offer of $54,000 with $2,000 cash now and the rest when we sell the property in three months. Our written offer may be for only $52,000 with $1,000 cash up front, which will allow us a few thousand dollars negotiating room before everything is accepted in triplicate.

WRITING UP THE OFFER

There are two schools of thought on the subject of writing an offer to purchase, and we've attended both. In the first, everything is left to professionals and the attitude is, "Don't make a move without your attorney." The second school is for the do-it-yourselfers, in which you brew your own home-cooked contract, complete with a dozen or more escape clauses.

If you're wondering which we recommend, you'll be

happy to know that we sit squarely on both sides of the issue. The advantages and disadvantages of each have convinced us that a middle-of-the-road philosophy is best.

Actually, there are many gradations between putting yourself in the hands of an attorney and doing everything by yourself. You can have a less expensive expert, such as a title officer, an investor, or a Realtor, help you fill in the blanks.

We suggest starting with training wheels and working your way up to independence. In other words, take full advantage of a real estate attorney's expertise the first time you buy property. You can graduate to the title officer (whose advice won't be legally binding) on the second transaction, and by the third or fourth purchase you'll be ready to assemble your own contracts.

FINDING AN ATTORNEY

You wouldn't hire the family doctor to perform open-heart surgery. Likewise, you shouldn't hire a general attorney to help you buy investment real estate. Instead, take the time to find a qualified real estate attorney.

There are at least two sources for locating this aristocrat of your investing team: referrals from other investors and, naturally, the Yellow Pages which you've dog-eared by now.

If you didn't join an investment group when we brought up the subject in an earlier chapter, do so now. Find a couple of active real estate investors and ask them for suggestions. If they've had any luck at all in finding a knowledgeable real estate lawyer they should be happy to pass along a reference.

The Yellow Pages will list attorneys under their specialties. You can usually get a free first-time consultation, which will allow you to shop for your own counsel without risk or obligation.

A back-up source of information is the Martindale-

Hubbell Law Directory, a fairly complete list of attorneys giving information on most of the lawyers in any given area. It will include such data as the year each one graduated from law school (and where he attended); whether or not he is a member of the American Bar Association. Furthermore, it will rate each attorney on the basis of ability and experience.

While the Martindale-Hubbell Law Directory isn't necessarily the last word, it is a good general indicator of the value of an attorney's services. A local law-school library or large central library should have a copy.

Once you've found an attorney who seems to be knowledgeable and experienced, and one you feel comfortable working with, sit down and outline everything you've been through and everything you want to accomplish. Like your psychiatrist or hairdresser, your lawyer can't advise you until he knows your case intimately. If you have a question, ask it. If you have an objection, voice it. If you want to take notes, do it. The object is to avoid paying that $100 per hour fee more than once. And if you pay close attention the first time you may be able to get by with minimal assistance in the future.

An experienced real estate attorney will be an absolute must when you begin your career in foreclosure investing. There are hundreds of laws governing foreclosures, and those laws change almost daily and vary widely from state to state, making a lawyer indispensable, at least the first time you buy.

OTHER EXPERTS

Full-time Realtors have extensive experience in helping buyers write their offers. By now you've no doubt established a close relationship with at least one competent real estate agent (right?) Ask your friend to help you fill out the purchase offer form.

Another expert, one that you will be using more and more as you approach the settlement, is a title officer. In many states closings can take place in a title office, and a title officer, whose job description will be given in detail shortly, can be a great help.

Successful investors, those few local real estate tycoons with a dozen deals in the belts, are often happy to help a struggling novice. They will have the experience necessary to play fill-in-the-blanks with you, and they may even have a few clauses you can use to protect yourself.

PURCHASE OFFER FORM

There are two basic purchase offer forms readily available. One is the garden-variety type, for sale in a stationery store. The second is the purchase offer form used by the local board of Realtors. Typically, the Realtors' form is the more comprehensive of the two. Since the name of the game is to protect yourself from every angle, we suggest that you use the form approved by your own local board of Realtors. Your best friend, the Realtor, can help you get a copy.

For the most part the forms are self-explanatory. But if you need a quick lesson in what to write in the spaces, the Realtor on your team can help you with the specifics.

You can look at the filled-in example from the previous chapter for a quick lesson in what to write in the spaces, and your resident expert can help you with the specifics.

IMPORTANT CLAUSES

We suggest that you add a few clauses to protect yourself in case you have to back out of the agreement prior to the closing:

" . . . and/or assigns."
We've already mentioned this once, but it belongs here and can't be over-stressed. This tiny tidbit of legal protection allows the purchaser to transfer his or her interest in the contract prior to the day of closing. If you can find a buyer before you actually buy the property, it's a simple matter to assign the lease and take your profit without ever owning the property.

"Offer subject to buyer's partner's approval."
This ingenuous-sounding clause is an escape hatch roughly the size of an airplane hangar door. Without encouraging unethical behavior, we'll make the observation that your partner can be anyone at all, from your business partner to your best friend's next-door neighbor's second cousin in Milwaukee. If, for any reason, you should decide to rescind your offer, you can do so by having your partner disapprove.

We have never bought a property without having at least two partners involved, and we counsel you to always ask for a second opinion from an experienced investor—who can act as your partner if you decide to withdraw from the agreement.

"Offer subject to . . ."
You can make your offer subject to more than just your partner's approval. It can be subject to everything from your ability to secure financing at a specified rate, for a specified amount, under specified terms, etc.

An acceptable, commonly used clause makes the offer subject to the property appraisal not being less than a specified amount, or insisting that the appraisal be within a certain percentage of the offer price. Another clause that works well is to make the offer subject to the property passing inspection by a variety of professionals, from a termite inspector to an electrical contractor or a plumber.

Most offers will include the clause mentioned just above, in which the offer is made subject to the buyer's ability to finance the purchase. For example, "Offer subject to buyer obtaining a loan for $65,000, fully amortized over 30 years, at an annual interest rate not to exceed 9.0 percent." This financing clause can be followed by a specific request for a refund of your security deposit in the case of failure to obtain acceptable financing.

Other subject-to's include: Offer subject to seller delivering a deed of good and clear record and marketable title. Exceptions must be clearly noted. Offer subject to the property conforming to zoning regulations and building codes.

All of these clauses are inserted by the buyer to protect his or her interest. They may be added to the body of the contract or attached as a separate addendum (review our example in the previous chapter). Your attorney can help you in adding clauses and may have a few more to add. But be forewarned that some owners can be scared of too many add-on clauses.

There isn't anything more to the written offer. Your local expert, whether it's an attorney, Realtor, title officer, or other mentor, will help you with the fine details. There are several elements that go into creating a quality contract. To make it easier to protect yourself, you should run through the following checklist when writing your own contract:

CONTRACT CHECKLIST

Make sure your contract contains all of the following:

1) A complete legal property description, not just the street address. In our case-study example we used only the common address, but we recommend that you take the trouble to look up the legal description in the county plat map.

You can get help looking it up from personnel in the county courthouse.

2) A complete list of all restrictions, covenants, and easements, as they are understood by the seller, and the seller must warrant that there are no restrictions, covenants, or easements that he or she is aware of that are not listed. Restrictive covenants may prohibit the use of property for a specific purpose; easements may allow the use of the property for purposes that you are unaware of, such as Farmer Brown next door having the right to drive his herd through your back yard every morning at four a.m.

3) A list of all liens and encumbrances that the buyer is aware of, with a warrant that to the best of the seller's knowledge there are no other liens or encumbrances. During the closing period (from the time the contract is signed until the transaction is settled) the buyer will conduct a title search to uncover any hidden liens; if any are uncovered, you may want to pull out of the deal.

4) A list of anticipated costs, and an agreement as to how they will be paid. These costs may include inspections, surveys, closing costs, title search and insurance, and other assorted expenses. While it is generally the buyer's responsibility to pay for inspections, appraisals, and the like, any agreement between the parties to divvy up the various obligations can be made.

5) An agreement by the seller to maintain the property in good condition until the closing date, and a provision whereby the buyer has the right to inspect the property within the last day or two before the closing. Without such a clause you may take possession to a disaster.

6) A list of all personal property that is to be included in the sale. Specify make, model, and even model number. We've heard a dozen horror stories of the 16 cubic-foot

refrigerator turning into an ancient icebox the night before the closing. It's surprising what items turn from fixtures to personal property at the last minute. List everything that isn't permanently affixed to the house. As an added bonus, you can insist in the contract that all appliances will be in good condition at the time of sale and up to 30 days after the sale.

7) The phrase "time is of the essence." These five words, to a lawyer or judge, mean that the contract is a timely agreement; that is, you won't allow lallygagging on the part of the sellers. The contract will become stale and worthless if you have to wait a year to close the deal.

When time is of the essence, the time periods stipulated in the contract are to be taken literally, and not merely as guidelines.

8) A description of how you intend to take title to the property. If you have a partner or spouse who will be involved in the purchase you will either take title as joint tenants or as tenants in common. Joint tenants own equal and undivided interest in the property, with a right of survivorship. If either partner dies, the other becomes the sole owner. Tenants in common hold separate, undivided interests, which can be passed on to heirs or transferred without the approval of the other party.

You can also take title as a sole owner, or a "tenant in fee." In such a case you are the absolute owner of the property and can sell, transfer, deed, or pass it on to your heirs as you see fit.

9) Specify the amount of your *earnest money* or security deposit, as well as the form in which it is to be paid and the party to whom you will make it payable. Do not give a penny more that you have to, and make it payable only to a title company, attorney, or Realtor. Under no circumstances should it be in the form of cash or a check payable to the

sellers. If the deal collapses prior to closing and you've covered yourself with an escape clause, you will have the legal right to reclaim your deposit. If you've made that deposit in cash to the sellers, you may not see it this side of a courtroom.

10) Give the sellers only one day to accept your offer. This may sound harsh, but experience has shown that the longer owners are given to consider the terms of your offer, the more likely they are to counteroffer. If they can't decide within 24 hours, after all the preliminary negotiating you've done, then they aren't really ready to sell.

11) Review the contract. Is everything clearly spelled out? Are you satisfied with the terms? Can you understand every clause? (There is no reason a contract can't be written in plain English.) If you feel that you've left bases uncovered, go back and cover them.

If you're using an attorney, he or she should already be an expert when it comes to contracts, and all of these particulars and more will be protected.

PRESENTING THE OFFER

You've done everything, you've planned, inspected, negotiated. You've written up an airtight contract. All you have to do is hand it to the sellers and get their signatures. For many first-time buyers it's the last psychological hurdle they have to clear. From this point on everything seems to take care of itself.

When you present the offer, do so with a confident, almost conspiratorial, smile and a warm handshake. Don't sit there on the edge of a kitchen chair nervously awaiting a response; leave the contract and explain that you'd like to give them time to look it over. You can add, on the way out the door, that you're looking forward to getting everything wrapped up.

There isn't much more to worry yourself sick over. Either they will sign, or make a counteroffer, or refuse your offer completely. In foreclosure situations the third alternative is rarely the case. If they make a counteroffer, it's up to you to review it and decide whether or not you can live with it. If you can, you're on your way to owning your first investment property.

ESCROW
The period between the time both parties have signed the offer and the day of the actual closing is called the *escrow period*. It's called the *settlement*, in many states. If you've ever purchased any real estate, including your own home, you should be familiar with this treacherous stage. Many deals fall through during escrow, for a variety of reasons. If you've left yourself enough escape clauses you should be able to cancel during escrow without losing your deposit, but in most cases the seller will be bound to the sale.

The escrow, technically, begins when the seller entrusts the deed to a third party (an attorney, title officer, loan officer, or other person or corporation) with the instructions that the deed is to be given to the buyer only after certain conditions have been met. The escrow holder opens an escrow account to keep track of all escrow funds, and issues a set of instructions to the buyer and seller, outlining their respective responsibilities prior to the closing.

The escrow period only needs to be long enough to do everything that needs to be done. During escrow you will need to arrange for financing, if financing is needed. You will also want to have the title searched, and you should obtain title insurance. You may have the property surveyed and inspected, in keeping with the terms of the contract.

If there is a foreclosure involved, and the sale date is only days away, you'll have to act extremely fast, and you may have to forego some of these steps.

Let's take a closer look at what occurs during escrow.

Financing

We've already discussed working with bankers in some detail. When the time comes to shop for a loan you should already have laid the groundwork by talking to the beneficiary involved in the sale. Keeping her need for security and return on investment in mind at all times, you can begin your negotiation for mortgage money.

Real estate finance is complex, confusing, and constantly changing. Entire books have been devoted to financing, and we couldn't do the subject justice without spending at least a chapter on it. Rather than do so, we recommend the following course of study:

1) Have several experts, including bankers, mortgage brokers, Realtors, and local investors sit down with you and explain various loan programs that are available. You should have a rather thorough understanding of current loan programs, which change from month to month.

2) Study mortgage financing. Two recommended readings: "The Common-Sense Mortgage," by Peter G. Miller (Harper & Row); and "The Real Estate Finance Tool Kit," a complete home-study course on the subject available through the Freedom Foundation, PO Box 796, Provo, Utah 84603.

3) In any foreclosure situation, discuss with the beneficiary the possibility of assuming the existing loan. Many loans contain a "due-on-sale clause," which states that the entire balance of the loan may be called due by the lender upon the sale of the property. Banks do not have to exercise this clause and they may be willing to forego doing so to save themselves the trouble of a foreclosure.

148

Nothing is an adequate substitute for study. Take a week to study up-to-date programs available from different institutions before you take out a loan anywhere. Back up your application with evidence that you won't default on the loan. Convince the lender that you're a good risk and you'll get the financing every time.

Title Search

The "chain of title" is the property's diary. Anyone can research this chain, which includes every lien, encumbrance, and ownership record listed in the county courthouse. Title companies make their money by researching chains of title, and a title officer can be one of your greatest allies. They tend to be quite knowledgeable about real estate, from how to fill out a purchase offer to what to expect at the closing. In many states the closing can take place in the title office, supervised by your title officer.

You will have determined which party is responsible for the title search. Once it has been researched, the title company will prepare an *abstract of title*, which is a complete list of the chain of title. If the seller isn't required to, you may (although it is not required, in most cases) pay for title insurance, by which the title company states that there are no hidden defects (or "clouds") on the title. The title insurance company agrees to defend the owner of the insurance against undiscovered defects.

In foreclosure situations it becomes a matter of more than casual interest to insure the title. Owners in trouble with one lender will often have trouble with other creditors, and a hidden tax lien for $50,000 could take the starch out of your day.

The length of time required for the search, and the cost of insurance or an abstract of title, will vary from one locale to another. Find out how much time you'll need before you write the contract.

Inspections, Surveys, Appraisals
Any or all of the three may be deemed advisable by your attorney and may even be mandated by your lender. None of them are free, but they are generally well worth the expense, particularly the first time you buy real estate.

If any professional inspection or appraisal turns up a defect, and if you've allowed yourself an escape clause, you can disappear unscathed. If nothing turns up, consider it part of your investment cost and buy the property.

One note about inspections and appraisals, which we made in passing earlier: Ask appraisers and inspectors if they will allow you to tag along. The education is invaluable.

If everything goes without a hitch, you only have one more chore: a last-day inspection before the closing. Walk through slowly, taking your time. If the seller's haven't already relocated (something you'll have to work out with them in advance), you can walk through with them and mutually agree that everything is ship-shape. If there are problems, ensure that the sellers realize that the entire deal is in jeopardy.

If the hatches are all battened, you're in business. The next step is the last, and certainly the most impressive, in a long series of steps that started when you first saw that notice of sale.

THE CLOSING
The formal closing is a somber, business-like affair in which the buyer, the seller, the buyer's agent or attorney, the seller's agent or attorney, and the escrow holder (banker, title officer, escrow company officer) are all present and

accounted for. With appropriately solemn expressions on their faces, the principles pass paperwork back and forth, signing here and there. When the signing is finished the seller will have his money and the buyer will own the property.

Where the closing takes place is a matter of agreement and custom. In many Eastern states it customarily takes place either in the seller's attorney's office or in the office of the buyer's lender. In Western states it will occur in the office of the escrow company or title company. In some instances it won't take place at all—the parties will exchange paperwork through the mail. However, this dismal development in the closing game takes all the fun and pomp out of buying real estate.

To prepare for the closing you should know in advance exactly what your closing costs will be. Some time antecedent to the meeting you will receive a list of anticipated closing costs, and shortly—as shortly as the day before—you will be given a Uniform Settlement Statement, in which you will be told exactly how much money you must bring to the settlement. You'll need to have a cashier's check—trust isn't an inherent part of any real estate transaction—to pay for all closing costs, including the money you owe the seller for his or her equity.

The following is a partial list of closing costs that you can expect to pay. The costs can be divided between the yourself and the seller as you see fit. However, in a foreclosure situation it is generally the buyer who gets stuck with the lion's share.

Points

A "point" is one percent of any loan, and you can expect to pay points every time you borrow money. For example, if you borrowed $70,000 with three points, you would have to pay three percent, or $2,100, to the lender, in cash at the closing. Points will vary from one location to another and from one lender to the next, so shop around before you agree to any loan.

For lenders, points are simply a few extra dollars to cover the loss of selling your loan to a third party, such as Fannie Mae (who we will discuss in a later chapter). Points are prepaid interest, a cost of borrowing money, and a necessary evil. If a lender offers a loan without points, it will be at a higher interest rate, so the choice will always be pay the interest now or later.

The lender will also charge a "loan origination fee," a bureaucratic euphemism for "more money we want to charge you for borrowing from us." Consider it another cost of borrowing money and compare prices before you sign.

Prorated Expenses

At the time title is transferred there will be several expenses that will pass from seller to buyer, such as taxes, insurance, interest on mortgages, city services, and utilities—to name a few.

Proration is the process whereby each expense is divided between the buyer and seller so that each is responsible for his share only as long as he owned the property.

While tradition dictates that such expenses will be prorated as of the day of escrow, the actual date can be set earlier or later, according to agreement.

Appraisal Fee

If you took our advice and used the services of an independent appraiser, you'll have to pay the appraisal fee. This fee can be made due and payable at the time of closing.

Transfer Fee

Each state charges its own fee for the transfer of title. This charge is, of course, just another chance for the government to get a sticky finger into your business, and there's no help for it. In most states it will be based on the value of the property, and you can find out well in advance how much you will pay.

Escrow Fees

Whoever is conducting the escrow is unlikely to be running a charity. They will charge for their services, and they will base that charge on the selling price. It pays to shop for escrow companies before committing yourself. Fees can range widely and competition can be fierce.

Title Insurance

Already discussed, you will likely have to bring a check to the closing to pay for the title insurance.

Lawyer's Fees

You will have an attorney, as will the seller and possibly the lender, and every one of them will have a manicured hand out at the closing table. The buyer and seller will each pay a portion of these odious obligations, which can range from under $100 to well over $500.

Commissions

If there is a Realtor involved, she is working for the seller, and paying the commission at closing is the seller's burden. However, in reality the extra cost is passed along to the buyer in the form of a higher purchase price.

Fortunately, in most foreclosures there won't be a Realtor involved by the time you find the property. If there is, you'll have to bring enough cash to the closing to cover the cost of the commission. Commissions traditionally run about six percent of the purchase price—on an $80,000 sale that translates to $4,800—in cash. No wonder investors prefer to bypass listed properties!

Impound Account

You will be required by the lender to prepay at least a month's taxes and a year's fire insurance, and, depending on the lender, much more. It makes sense that the lender wants you to pay in advance, to cover his bets for a month or two, but this charge can get expensive, and should be another consideration when you're shopping for money.

Other Charges

You may have to bring enough money to the closing to cover everything from a termite report to some unheard-of charge that the lender dreamed up in the middle of the night. All costs will be included in the list you will receive prior to closing.

After all the necessary mumbling, calculating, signing, and paying has been done, everyone will shake hands all around and congratulate each other. The seller will hand over the keys to the castle and you will officially join the ranks of the American capitalist real estate investors.

TAKING POSSESSION

In foreclosure situations it's not uncommon to have the sellers remain on the property for at least a brief period after the sale. They very likely might need proceeds from the sale itself to pay for the move. It's also possible to work out a rental arrangement, under which they could remain as renters for as long as you want them to stay.

In our example, we allowed Gus and Doreen, as a part of our agreement, to remain on the property for a month after the sale, rent free. Our expense was one month's rental payment, which we figured into the cost of owning the property. It didn't hurt us to have them there, taking care of the property, and when they left we were able to sell it quickly. They appreciated the one-month cushion. We appreciated their cooperation. And it surely beat a forcible eviction.

In every case where we've bought property before the auction, we've been able to work out a friendly move-out agreement that the sellers could live with. It's simply another factor to work out while you are negotiating the terms of the transaction.

Well, that's it. You own the property. Congratulations! Time to fix it up, if it needs it, and then either rent it or sell it. Jump ahead to Chapter 8.

The next two chapters deal with the alternatives to working with the owners: buying at the trustee's sale, and buying after the sale. Both are workable when there isn't enough equity to make working with the owners practicable, or when the owners are impossible to work with.

CHAPTER SIX

Buying At The Sale

Whether it's call it a foreclosure sale or a trustee's auction, it amounts to the same thing. If there is a power of sale, the mortgagee or the trustee will sell the property at public auction to the highest bidder.

With exceptions and rules that vary from state to state (and which you should familiarize yourself with by asking your real estate attorney), the course of the auction will be very much the same in every case, as described in Chapter 2. Other forced sales include tax sales, sherrif's sales, and court-supervised sales. We will cover tax sales briefly, but the other forced sales—especially the ones that drag the judiciary into the fray—are usually better left alone.

GOOD DEALS AT AUCTION

There is one criterion for what makes a "good deal" good that always applies, whether you buy from the owner before the auction, the trustee at the auction, or the beneficiary after the auction. There must be equity. It's the first commandment of buying real estate. Let's look at a couple of examples.

Example 1
The house has a market value of $82,000. The outstanding debt, including overdue payments and legal fees, total $80,500. Should you buy it before, during, or after the auction, or should you forget it entirely?
It's a trick question. You can't tell from the information given. It's fairly obvious that working with the owner would be a waste of time and money. We're talking about an owner in serious trouble. If he does manage to sell at market value he'll have to pay off the existing debt, leaving barely enough to cover his half of the closing costs. And for you, the buyer, paying $82,000 means no equity and no "great deal."
You can buy at auction if there is enough equity available. And equity at the sale depends on how the various liens stack up. Let's break Example 1 down into two possible scenarios:

Scenario 1
There are three liens. Lien A is a first mortgage with a current balance of $58,000. Overdue payments and assorted fees add another $2,000, for a total of $60,000. The mortgagee (or beneficiary) of lien A is foreclosing.
Lien B is a second mortgage with a balance of $18,000. The property owner has been making his payments, so there is nothing overdue and no penalties.
Lien C is a mechanic lien for $2,500.
To make things easier, look at the accompanying summary.
This situation has potential. The second and third lienholders may not show up for the sale, in which case you can buy the property for $60,001, picking up $22,000 equity at the sale. Of course, they may protect their interests, or the second lienholder may show up and the third may not, and you can buy the property for as little as $78,001. You would

Scenario 1

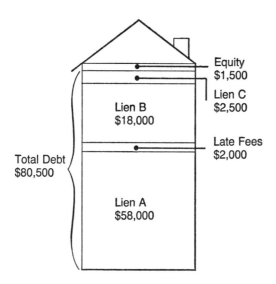

have $4,000 instant equity, which may or may not be enough to justify the purchase.

If all three lienholders show up and bid, you'll have to put in your two cents—or, rather, your $80,501. If that happens, you're back to square one, with no equity.

With proper prior planning you might just swing a good deal in this situation, as we'll describe shortly when we get into strategies for buying at the sale, but we don't want to tip our hand here. Instead, let's consider the next scenario.

Scenario 2

There is only one lien. The beneficiary will make a non-cash bid of $80,500. If you want to buy at auction you'll have to bid $80,501. Back to the drawing board.

Scenario 2

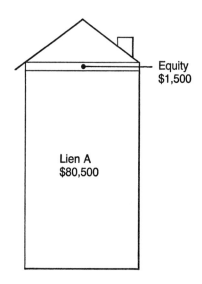

Equity
$1,500

Lien A
$80,500

Example 2

Second house, similar to the first in that the market value is $82,000. However, the financing is very different. The total liens equal only $60,000. Three liens again: A, B, and C. Lien A has a balance of $32,500; lien B is $3,000; lien C takes up the rest at $24,500.

A good deal? Almost certainly. Even if all three lienholders show up, you can outbid them and pick up the property for as little as $60,001—if there isn't any competition. Also, you can use a technique that we'll show later in this chapter to put a couple thousand dollars in your pocket without ever owning the property.

Example 2

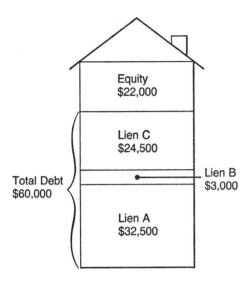

We could go through a second scenario, with only one lien of $60,000, but the picture remains the same. If there is no competition from other investors, you can outbid the beneficiary and buy the property for $60,001.

As you can see, equity is the only rule for buying at auction. With a few hours invested into researching the property you can determine whether or not you have a money-making opportunity long before the day of sale.

PROS AND CONS

Before you show up with your briefcase full of money, you should understand that buying real estate at a trustee's sale can be a perilous undertaking. There are professional buyers there who do nothing else, and many of them earn enough to make the monthly payment on the Rolls, but more than one naive investor has been badly burned after the auction.

As a perfect example of how well things can go when they go well, we bought a property at auction not long ago, paying only $47,500 for a house valued at $69,000. There were three liens against the property, with balances of approximately $43,000, $8,000, and $4,500. We knew, from researching, that the third lienholder wouldn't even show up for the sale. They were ready to write off the $4,500, rather than having to buy the property (paying cash for the first and second mortgages) and resell it.

The second lienholder probably would have put in a bid, just to protect their $8,000, but we contacted them prior to the sale and offered to buy the lien at a discount. They accepted our offer (we were saving them from the trouble of getting involved in a foreclosure sale), and all we had to do was outbid the beneficiary, who was happy to be rid of the headache.

We put that one in our trophy case, but it sits there alone. Our experience has been that great auction buys like that are few and far between.

The plus side of buying at auction is that the junior liens, if they aren't protected by their holders, are wiped out, freeing up instant equity. Also the sale is cut and dried—you bring the cash, you make your bid, and, if you win, you get a trustee's deed immediately. It beats the red tape usually involved in a real estate transaction.

On the downside? Well, we'll describe them:

"As is."
When you buy at auction, you get the very minimum title of a trustee's deed. You purchase the property as is, with

absolutely no warranties. If you find out that the previous owner was an insane cheese collector who kept his walls stuffed with Limburger, and you can't get rid of the stuff, too bad. Tough luck if the heater is faulty and the place burns to the ground.

"Subject to . . ."

You also take title subject to every existing senior lien, hidden or not. If Uncle Sam holds a tax lien that you were unaware of, you're stuck with it. If the second lienholder forecloses, and the first lien is a non-assumable mortgage held by Shyster Savings and Loan, you may have a problem with the people at Shyster.

The following is a list of potential problems that you might inherit along with ownership:

Due-on-sale Clauses

When bankers experienced their near disaster in the late 1970s, it didn't take them long to figure out a few new tricks. One of them was the dreaded *due-on-sale clause*. This clause puts the lender in the driver's seat whenever the property is sold by giving him the right to qualify the buyer, raise the interest rate, or, in some cases, call the entire principal balance due.

In the case of a foreclosure, if the second mortgage is foreclosed on and the first contains a due-on-sale clause, the buyers at auction may have to qualify to assume the first mortgage. If they fail to do so, the entire balance may be due. If they do qualify, the interest rate (and therefore the payment) may be adjusted upward.

Most conventional loans made after 1978 do contain a due-on-sale clause, and should be approached with caution. Pre-1978 conventional loans, as well as FHA and VA loans

163

are fully assumable.

Whenever you buy property—foreclosure or not—watch for the due-on-sale clause. If, in your eagerness to become a wealthy investor, you ignore this one point and then fail to qualify for the loan, the lender will foreclose.

Balloon Mortgages

A balloon mortgage is any mortgage or trust deed that calls for a large lump-sum payment at a future date. Many properties facing foreclosure are in trouble *because* of a balloon mortgage. Reinstating such a loan would require that the entire loan balance be paid.

Often a balloon mortgage is in second or third position, held by a private individual, such as the previous owner. If the first is foreclosing, you may want to get the balloon mortgage holder to sell his or her interest to you at a discount, giving you a Satisfaction of Mortgage. Then you can reinstate the first mortgage and foreclose, or bid at the auction.

Acceleration Clauses

Most mortgages and trust deeds contain an acceleration clause. This is another self-preservation clause installed by lenders to protect their interests. It allows the lender to foreclose on the entire unpaid principal balance, not just the amount in arrears. In effect, it calls for the repayment schedule to be "accelerated."

There is no need to search for a mortgage without an acceleration clause; they are a standard part of the contract.

Do not assume that if you don't hear from the first and second mortgage holders they have forgotten about it! It is your responsibility to contact senior lenders and take care of assuming those obligations. There is a joke just for foreclosure specialists: Do you want to get involved in foreclosures? Just quit making your house payments. You'll be involved in a foreclosure in no time at all.

Competition

Example time again. You've found a property with two liens against it. The first beneficiary is foreclosing on a $46,000 trust deed, and the second is only $5,000. The property has a market value of at least $85,000. You can probably buy it for as little as $46,001, fix it up, sell it, and clear nearly $20,000.

What a deal! Until you show up for the auction, where you have to shoulder your way past 30 other investors.

Even if only two investors show up, the bidding will surely drive the price close to market value, as each successive bid shaves another hundred dollars off the profit.

Competition will be especially heated in a metropolitan area, where hundreds of foreclosure investors may show up to make a fortune. The great foreclosure deals are likely to be found in out-of-the-way areas and smaller towns. However, in any locale there may be a real threat from friends and associates of the trustee, the beneficiary, even the foreclosed owner.

If there is no equity to be bought at the sale—and in the majority of sales this is true—then you won't want to bid. If there is plenty of equity, the property will usually never make it to auction, and if it does there will be competition.

Cash

Auctions are cash-on-the-barrelhead deals. In most states the winning bidder will only have a matter of a few hours to pay the entire bid price in cash or a cashier's check. In some states a good-faith security deposit will be acceptable for a few days, but the balance must be paid when the trustee's deed is prepared.

You have three alternatives: your own bank account, a partner (or partners), or a loan. The first is self-explanatory. The other two options will be discussed shortly. Weighing the pros against the cons, the cons seem to be tipping the scales in their favor. But that doesn't mean you can't make money buying at the auction, as our example proves. It merely means that you must buy with both eyes open.

BUYING AT AUCTION

If you're still determined to buy at the trustee's sale, we'll help you all we can. In the following pages we'll walk through a sale with you, teach you a strategy for making money at the sale without buying, tell you where to get the cash you'll need, and give you a few pointers to get you started.

Before the Sale

You can't just show up at the sale without having done any background study. Well, you can, but it's like driving blindfolded—you're just asking for trouble.

You will have already attempted to contact the owner. Therefore, you should have inspected the property, determined its market value, and have had a title search done. (Before any lending institution will finance you, they will insist on a title search.) You will know exactly how many liens exist, the amount of each. You will know how much equity is available.

You should know which lienholders are likely to show up for the auction, so you'll know in advance how much will be bid. (You can contact the trustee prior to sale to find out exactly how much will be required to cover the lien being foreclosed.) The junior lienholders, if they haven't filed for notice of default, may be unaware of the foreclosure.

At the Auction

We've already discussed the sale itself in some detail. The auction will be held in a public place. The trustee will handle the entire proceeding and take bids. In nine out of ten cases, the beneficiary will be the only party that shows up to bid. Junior claimants with large enough liens will outbid senior claimants to protect their interests.

If you know in advance that there will be equity worth bidding for, come prepared with a cashier's check for your bid.

If you are the highest bidder, you will tender the cash to the trustee, who will pay the beneficiary and turn the rest over to an equity court for disbursements to junior lienholders and the former owner. The property is yours, subject to any liens and encumbrances that were senior to the one being foreclosed.

There isn't any more to it. If you've done your research carefully and thoroughly, you know exactly what you've bought. If you haven't accounted for any existing prior liens, or if you've miscalculated the property's actual market value, your investment may not pay off as handsomely as you would have hoped. Some buyers at auction will actually lose money. But that's because they failed to study the case well enough in advance.

After the Sale

The trustee will prepare a trustee's deed for you. It is a deed to the property, which must be recorded. Having paid the trustee, the property is now yours. You should have already contacted the prior lienholders regarding the assumability of their loans. If they are assumable, you will have to ensure that your name appears on the paperwork. Otherwise, the previous owner may be billed for the payments, and when he fails to pay them you may find yourself involved in another foreclosure—with you as the "foreclosee."

You will have had a thorough title search done before the sale. After the sale you can get title insurance based on that search. Contact your title officer and by all means pay the extra price of an insurance premium. If there is an undiscovered prior lien, the title company will be held liable.

Assignment of a Lien

You don't have to buy the property to make money at the sale. There is at least one strategy, called *assigning the junior liens*, that can put money in your pocket every time, with almost no risk and no money.

We've already mentioned the idea once or twice. Let's take a closer look. There are cases in which a junior claimant may not be willing or able to come to the auction to protect his or her interest. Study this example:

Market Value	$100,000
Equity	45,000
2nd—Judgment	5,000
1st—Savings & Loan	50,000

In this situation, the holder of the second lien, or judgment, would have to bid over $50,000 cash to salvage his or her claim. Despite the high equity involved, the judgment creditor may be unable to put up the necessary cash and therefore may be ready to write off the $5,000 as a loss. An investor, seeing an opportunity, will offer the judgment holder $1,000 for the "worthless" judgment.

With the high equity involved, the actual bidding should exceed $55,000, and when the court disburses the excess money to the junior lienholders, the investor, having bought the judgment for $1,000, will pocket a $4,000 profit. As another example of the same principle, study the accompanying diagram.

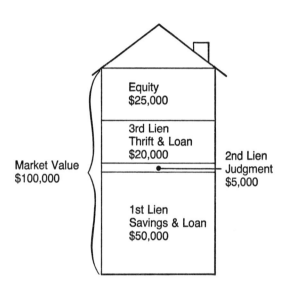

In this example, Savings & Loan is foreclosing. Thrift & Loan will certainly show up, to protect its $20,000 interest, but it only needs to bid $50,001 to take the property . . . unless you show up, having paid $1,000 for an assignment of the judgment. You will bid $55,000, to cover your own interest, and Thrift & Loan, whose lien would be wiped out, will be forced to bid $55,001. When they do so, the trustee (or court) will pay you $5,000 for your judgment.

Buying junior liens at a discount isn't a common occurrence, of course, but it is frequent enough that with a little pre-sale homework an investor can turn a very quick profit.

If you're still awake, a question may have arisen: "Why wouldn't a junior claimant have simply reinstated the loan within the 90-day NOD period, rather than discount his interest to me?" There are three basic reasons:

1) Lack of knowledge.
2) Lack of time.
3) Lack of money.

First, many people who hold a junior position are unaware of the risk they face when a senior loan is in default. Furthermore, they are unaware that they have a unique right, as a junior lienholder, called the *endangered collateral rule*, that allows them to reinstate the senior lien and foreclose themselves. Oblivious to the danger, they wait too long to protect their position.

Second, foreclosure takes time. Many junior claimants are not only unaware of the foreclosure process, but they simply haven't the time to pursue their interests. Distance is sometimes a factor; the previous seller is often a junior claimant, having accepted a second or third position on a carried-back loan. They may be living a thousand miles away, unable to protect their mortgage long distance.

Third, reinstating a loan takes cash. If the loan is three months in arrears, the total fee may be $3,000 or more on even a small loan. If the junior claimant can't scrape up enough cash, he has no choice but to wait for the day of the sale and hope the winning bidder covers his lien.

The point is, there are always cases where junior claimants are put in a losing position, and rather than fight for their interests, they will be happy—well, maybe not happy, but willing—to sell out their position to a investor.

FINDING THE MONEY

We've been here once before, haven't we? Once again we'll try to borrow up to $100,000 cash, from a partner or a banker, and we might only have a couple of days to do it.

Partners

The first source, which we covered in some detail earlier, is a private investor—or a collective of partners—who will put up the cash. The trick is in convincing your partners that you've got a red-hot opportunity of a lifetime. To do that you'll need a proposal that answers your partners' questions before they are asked.

The form the proposal takes is up to you, but it must include information that your partners will be looking for: return on investment security and a specific plan for buying and selling the property.

We strongly suggest using a computer. If you aren't using a computer at this point, invest in one. We're living in the computer age. If you don't own a computer it's only because you haven't yet realized its potential as an investment tool. You don't drive a horse and buggy, and you surely don't use a slide rule for calculating. A computer with a printer and software for real estate investing will pay for itself quickly.

Getting back to the main subject, your proposal should list the property by address, its history, a complete list of liens (and their outstanding balances), the proposed purchase price, the market value, and a complete selling strategy. It should break down the numbers, including all closing costs, anticipated profit, and just about anything you can think of, so your partners can see at a glance what they are buying.

If there is enough equity to assure your partner a high enough return to beat alternative investments, and if you've assembled an attractive proposal, you won't have trouble finding willing partners. You can even divide the deal between more than one partner. There's no law that prevents you from bringing in a thousand partners at $100 apiece.

Conventional Lenders

We're back in the banker's territory, this time to ask for $80,000 cash. To use this strategy, you must be able to show your favorite lender (are you developing a good relationship with a banker?) that:

□ The property is definitely going to be sold at auction.
□ There is substantial equity to be acquired at the sale.
□ If the bank lends you the money it will be well protected.

A property with a market value of $90,000 goes to auction. The first mortgage holder is foreclosing on a loan of $55,000 and there is a second lien against the property for $12,000. How can you, as an investor with little or no cash, buy the property?

Existing liens total $67,000, leaving equity of $23,000. Visit your loan officer and ask for a loan of $70,000—contingent on your ability to purchase the property for less than that amount. Have your lender escrow the money with your title company, with a letter of instruction that the funds may be disbursed only in the event that you are the successful bidder at the trustee's sale and that the amount bid is less than the funds held in escrow. If the trustee will accept a trust account check drawn on the title company, you will not need a certified check. If the trust check isn't acceptable, you will usually have a few hours in which to get a cashier's check.

The title company will probably send a representative with you to the trustee's sale, to verify that you complied with the conditions of the loan. The title company's check will be tendered to the trustee on your behalf and the title company will then be able to disburse the funds held in escrow.

Having bought the property for $70,000, you can easily sell it for $80,000, paying off your loan and putting $10,000 in the bank. If you have done the proper research well in advance, you should be able to get the loan based on the equity available, and you've made an incredible nothing-down profit.

GOING ONCE, GOING TWICE

Do your homework, plan your strategy, don't fall in love with the property, and don't get carried away. That, in a nutshell, is how to succeed at auction.

Before you ever make a bid, however, practice. Attend a few sales and observe. If you see something that doesn't make sense, ask someone who looks like he knows what he's doing. It wouldn't hurt to sit in on 10 sales or more before you raise your hand and join the squabble. You might want an expert—an experienced attorney, trustee, investor, etc.—to help you through the process the first time. After that, *you'll* be the expert.

Once you feel comfortable, do it. We've counseled would-be investors who stood on the sidelines for years, trying to work up the nerve to actually buy. On the other hand, Loretta was 24 when she bid on her first foreclosure property, and Carl was only 22. Don't wait until they pass out the Social Security checks to begin investing. As we've already mentioned, if you've done the necessary research you can feel perfectly confident in bidding.

TAKING POSSESSION

Rarely will the home still be occupied. The previous owners will have been made aware of the sale, if by no one else, at least by you. If the owners haven't vacated, you will

173

have to help them. That help can take any form you choose. However, the shotgun method lacks the social grace of, say, a polite reminder accompanied by a strict deadline.

When you've purchased a home at auction, you have the right to evict the possessors from your property. Exercising that right, however, can be risky business. Many of them will be bitter and will put up a fight. Some will willfully damage your property, and your right to sue them for damages is useless if they have no money or assets. If, after you have given them notice of eviction, they refuse to vacate the premises, you may have to call a sheriff, who will lend a helping hand.

A much better idea is to approach the old owners tactfully, with sincere consideration for their feelings. Convince them that you aren't Snidely Whiplash, trying to shove them forcibly into the raging blizzard. Explain that although you understand their plight, you have purchased the property and you will need to have them relocate as soon as possible. Ask them when they can be out, and set a very firm date with the understanding that if they cannot be out by that date, it will be necessary for you to have them forcibly evicted.

Helping the previous owners can entail giving them some financial assistance so they can get relocated as quickly and as painlessly as possible. If you've already been in contact with the owners, and have been watching the property, you'll know in advance how much trouble you may be facing. Plan ahead.

Perhaps the best advice is to not worry about what might happen. The fact is that 99 out of 100 times the previous owner will have long since flown to another coop, and possession is only a matter of turning the key and walking into your new house.

CHAPTER SEVEN

Buying After The Sale

The title of this chapter doesn't seem to make much sense. But then again, neither does "buying before the sale," and we already proved you could make a bundle before the sale.

Naturally, we're talking about buying from the winning bidder after the auction. In most cases that will be the beneficiary, who will have made a non-cash bid to take the property back.

To understand the idea better, consider this situation: The property is worth $90,000. The debt against it, including six months' back payments and various fees, totalled $88,000, and nobody showed up for the auction. You could have bought it yourself, but why buy a house worth $90,000 for $88,000?

Rather than do so, you can buy it from the bank for, say, $82,000, with excellent terms. Banks aren't real estate investors. They hate having to sell their foreclosure properties and they may be very glad to work with you.

REOs

An REO is a piece of real estate taken back by a lender in a foreclosure auction. REO is an acronym for "Real Estate Owned," which is how the property shows up on the bank's books. Every now and then a bank inspector drops by to look at the books, and if there are too many REOs it means trouble. The naughty banker has been making too many bad loans, and the inspector may have to tighten the bank's credit. Banks aren't crazy about inspectors, and they absolutely despise REOs.

In addition to accounting problems, REOs are heavy cash investments that earn nothing until they are sold. They require tax payments, upkeep, real estate commissions, and, since they are usually vacant, vandalism is a common problem. Let's face it—they are motivated sellers.

You can buy the property from the beneficiary immediately after the sale, even for the same price as the beneficiary paid for it. What's the advantage?

The beneficiary can clean up the property and any existing liens, and you can buy it with clear title. Many times the lender can strike a deal on the spot, right on the courthouse steps, and will consider himself lucky to do so. He avoids all of the problems mentioned above and you get twice the bargain for the same price.

REO might stand for "really excellent opportunities." To use another example, let's say there is a property in town with three liens against it. The first mortgage, for $65,000, is in foreclosure. The second, a paltry $12,000, will be wiped out at auction, as will the third, a $15,000 judgment (the junior lienholders can't afford the time, money, and hassle of buying the property at auction). The house is worth $95,000.

If you buy from the owners you'll have to pay $92,000, plus closing costs. If you buy at auction you'll have to outbid the first lienholder, paying $65,001 for a property in "as is" condition, subject to any undiscovered liens—and you'll have to pay in cash.

After the sale, however, you can buy it for the same $65,000 and insist that it be cleaned up—physically as well as fiscally. And, you can borrow the money from the beneficiary to buy it! It's no wonder many investors consider REOs the best source of foreclosure profits.

As you know, we're partial to buying before the auction, but if there isn't enough equity before the sale, REOs are often better than buying at auction.

BANKERS

There is only one drawback to working with bankers: working with bankers. If you're a banker, or related to one, please forgive us our impertinence. It's based on experience, and we're still looking for the perfect banker.

To meet your local banker, enter your local bank and ask for the officer in charge of REOs. Tell the REO officer that you are an investor who is interested in purchasing real estate from the bank.

The banker you speak to may or may not have the authority to sell you the property and extend a loan to cover the cost. Find out before you begin negotiating. If you have someone with the authority, ask to see a list of REO properties. If you're following a particular property through the entire foreclosure process, tell the banker what you already know about it.

Most banks will sell their properties through a real estate agent, and you may be referred to that agent; however, it's always best to buy directly from the bank if they will work with you. Real estate agents charge commissions, which will be passed along to you in the form of a higher price.

While we're on the subject of price: Most banks have a simple rule regarding price. They must sell property for at least the amount they have invested in it, including legal fees and real estate commissions. It's unlikely that they can sell it for much more, since banking regulations prohibit a bank from investing in real estate (although there are proposals in several states that would allow state-chartered banks to invest up to 10% of their assets in real estate).

Working with a bank after the sale isn't much different than working with one before the sale, except that now you are solving the bank's problem, rather than a private owner's. The banker will still want the same security she wanted before. She's already made one bad loan on the property; two would be unforgivable.

You already know the key to success, don't you? You need a winning combination of equity in the property and personal credit. If the bank can only sell the property for its market value—or close to it—forget it. If, however, there is equity available, you can use that as a selling point to get financing.

"The house on Elm street is worth $85,000, and your bank only has $68,000 invested in it. If you'll sell it to me for $70,000, and finance the purchase, you will have the security of $15,000 equity if I default—and I won't default; I'm in business to make money, not lose it."

If you've invested successfully before, you should have a portfolio that proves your mastery as a real estate investor. If you have any money at all, in checking, savings, or other accounts, transfer it to the bank you want to work with. If you have a plan for fixing up the property and selling it, share your plans with the banker. In other words, do anything you have to do to quell the banker's fear of making another bad loan.

You are the one behind the driver's seat, and don't forget it. If you don't buy the property, you haven't lost anything. If you make an offer and the REO officer rejects it, come back a month later and try again—the pressure of time is always on your side. If you want to push the issue, go over the loan officer's head, to the branch manager, a bank vice-president, or any other figure of authority. Or at least let the REO officer know you will do so. Remember who is saving whose hide; it's nice to be in control of a banking relationship for once.

Following a flood of foreclosures, there has to be a glut of REOs. Never have so many banks had so much real estate to sell. For investors it's a wonderful opportunity to make money after the auction.

OTHER REOs

Banks aren't the only ones trying to get rid of foreclosure properties. Any lienholder who "wins" at the sale will become the new-and-sometimes-unwilling owner. That includes private individuals, secondary mortgage companies, and the government. And they are all interested in selling.

Private Individuals

It's a rare day when a private lienholder takes a property in foreclosure and says "Goody!" They may have plenty to say, but we can't print it here.

Private, that is non-institutional, lienholders are usually previous owners who agreed to take back a second mortgage and were later forced to foreclose. They sold the old home once. They went through the hassle of fixing it up, advertising it (or listing it with a Realtor), and selling it, paying for at least half the closing costs. Now they've been through the trauma and expense of foreclosure. The last thing they want to do is get back into the selling game and go through all the bother a second time. And, maybe worst of all, they now realize that it could happen again and again.

If you've been following the sale from the beginning, you

can contact the lienholder right at the auction. Offer to buy the property for slightly more than they had to bid to take it back, and offer to cover all fix-up and closing costs (if there is enough equity to justify it).

Let's put it into numbers: The first owner, Lonnie Lienholder, sells her home (which she owns free and clear) to Sam Slick for $82,000. The market value of the house is about $83,000. Sam takes out a loan for $45,000 at Happy Valley Savings, enough to cover Lonnie's cash needs, and she takes back a second mortgage for $37,000.

Four years go by. Sam splits the scene, leaving Lonnie and Happy Valley Savings to foreclose. Happy Valley does so, and, to protect her interest, Lonnie covers Happy Valley's mortgage and forecloses herself, taking the property back.

Lonnie isn't a happy lady. She has the house back, but she had to shell out $43,000 or so to pay off Happy Valley, and to do so she had to take out a loan. Now she's making payments on a house she doesn't even want, which is sitting vacant, collecting dust. Sam stopped making payments on the second mortgage, which had a balance of $35,000 when he skipped town.

What kind of offer can you structure? Think about it for a minute before answering.

That was a minute?

Look at Lonnie's real needs, versus her wants. She wants to get full market value for the property, but at the same time she wants to sell this albatross. What she needs is at least $43,000 cash, to pay off the loan she took out to pay Happy Valley.

You can offer as little as $43,000, plus all closing costs, and she'll be better off than if she did nothing. However, your offer will be rejected.

You can offer full market value which will please Lonnie, but won't do much for your investing career. The best bet is somewhere in between. How far in between depends on Lonnie. A middle-ground offer of, say, $60,000 might be met with some interest, especially if you can prove to her that because of your expertise as a professional investor she'll never have to see that piece of property again. It will be even more attractive if Lonnie had moved a thousand miles away two weeks after she sold the house to Sam.

With some negotiating, and a guarantee that you'll make the whole process as painless as possible, Lonnie can be convinced that it's better to sell at a discount than to go through the torture of reselling. This way you can pick up $10,000 or more instant equity.

Secondary Lenders

There is a secondary mortgage market, wherein companies buy and sell mortgages. If you own a home, chances are the bank you borrowed from sold your loan to one of these companies.

The real biggie in the field is Fannie Mae (FNMA, the Federal National Mortgage Association), a privately-held corporation. Fannie Mae purchases mortgages from various lending institutions at a discount.

When the borrower of a Fannie Mae loan defaults, Fannie Mae ends up owning the property. Fannie Mae isn't any happier about owning an REO than any other lender. Fannie Mae is willing to deal.

You can get a list of all Fannie Mae foreclosures in any given area simply by calling 1-800-553-4636 (in Maryland, 1-800-221-4636). Phone lines are open 9 a.m. to 5 p.m. Eastern Time, Monday through Friday.

You can also obtain a list by writing to Fannie Mae

Properties, PO Box 13165, Baltimore, MD 21203. When you call or write, specify the approximate size of the property you're looking for (number of bedrooms, bathrooms, price range, etc.), as well as the general location. Fannie Mae will promptly send you a complete list of properties available in the specified area.

When you have found a Fannie Mae foreclosure property you're interested in buying, contact a local real estate agent. All Fannie Mae properties are sold through agents, and both the agent and Fannie Mae can assist you in financing the purchase.

FHA and VA Repossessions

The federal government, through the Federal Housing Administration (FHA) and Veterans Administration (VA), has insured loans on residential real estate. When you hear the term "FHA loan," or "VA loan," it doesn't mean the government actually loaned the money to the borrower. Instead, the government has agreed to insure the lender against default. Those loans haven't been immune to the tidal wave of default.

As a result, FHA and VA have found themselves burdened with an incredible stock of unwanted, vacant houses across the country. And they're willing to sell at a discount to be rid of them.

All FHA and VA repossessions are listed through real estate brokers. To get a list of homes, visit your Realtor friend and tell him or her that you're interested in buying a government "repo." You'll be treated to an afternoon on the town, driving from one empty house to the next.

Most FHA and VA repossessions are in poor shape, but with two day's work and a few hundred dollars they can become excellent rental properties. And, occasionally, there will be a spanking-new home available through FHA or VA. Many first-time home buyers find their first nest through this program.

You buy FHA and VA homes by sending in an offer, which the government will sagely consider for a few weeks before accepting or rejecting it. If they accept it they will require only five percent down, and will help you finance it through the very loan program that got them into trouble in the first place.

FHA and VA are run by government bureaucrats, so don't hold us to the terms outlined above. They change regulations and restrictions almost as often as a hotel changes its sheets, so they will likely have a new program by the time you're ready to buy. Your Realtor can explain the details.

IRS—Getting a Good Deal from Uncle Sam

If a property has a federal tax lien against it, and that property is foreclosed in a trustee's sale, the IRS will buy the property from the highest bidder, paying the amount bid plus a premium. Uncle Sam will then add in the amount of the tax lien and sell the property at public auction. If the trustee's sale price, plus the tax lien, is higher than the market value of the property, the price can be adjusted downward (the IRS apparently has enough money that it can afford to take a loss).

If you missed the trustee's sale, you can barter with the IRS after the trustee's sale and make a bid of your own on the upcoming IRS sale. You will be required to deposit 20% of your bid as a guarantee that you will bid at least the minimum set by the IRS. In the event you are outbid, your deposit will be refunded. If you win the bid, you will own the property.

No matter who you buy the property from, if you buy after the auction, you'll have to go through the normal buying procedure discussed in chapter 5, including qualifying for financing, getting title insurance, inspecting the property, and paying closing costs.

That's about it. The key, for the absolute last time, is *EQUITY*. If there is enough equity at the beginning to make it worthwhile, buy from the owner. If there isn't enough equity, wait for the sale and hope that the junior lienholders will drop out. If the auction isn't the place to buy, follow up and buy it from the beneficiary or the winning bidder. If there still isn't enough equity, forget it. Move on to the next deal. There are too many big fish in the sea to waste your time with minnows.

CHAPTER EIGHT

Fixing, Managing & Selling Your Properties

So now you own some real estate. Now what? Now comes the tough part: fixing, managing or selling it. In this chapter we'll teach you a few tricks of the trade, so you can turn that lovely equity into the real thing—cash profit.

FIXING YOUR PROPERTY

Fixing up property before selling it, especially foreclosure property, which may have been vacant for months, is a necessary evil. Fortunately, it doesn't have to cost more than a few hundred dollars, and it can often bring an extra thousand or more when you sell.

It's your responsibility to avoid buying real estate that needs a major facelift. The fixing up we're talking about involved such chores as:

□ Mowing.
□ Watering.
□ Weeding.
□ Painting the trim.
□ Professional carpet cleaning.
□ Paint touch-up.

□ Scrubbing the walls.
□ Replacing light bulbs throughout.
□ Cleaning all windows, mirrors, light fixtures.
□ Adding small extras, such as a new shower curtain.
□ Replacing dirty electrical wall plates.

You might want to take it a step further, if the return on your fix-up costs warrants it:
□ Planting new shrubs. Flower pots aren't expensive.
□ Get new carpet, as long as it's not needed throughout.
□ Repaint the exterior, which could get very expensive.
□ Repaint the interior, which is usually worth the investment.
□ Get new appliances. Possibly slightly used.
□ Do minor carpentry, plumbing, or electrical fix-ups.

You don't have to do the dirty work yourself. In fact, it often pays to bring in a professional house cleaner and a professional gardener for an afternoon. You could save a few dollars by doing the work yourself, but your time should be worth more than a few dollars, and a true professional will do a better job in half the time.

Avoid major repairs, such as a new roof or a new electrical system, and stay away from home-improvement projects such as swimming pools, which almost never pay for themselves.

The thing to watch when fixing up is an old rule of economics called the law of diminishing returns. Everything follows the same law, which in this case states that every dollar invested in fixing up a home will increase its value by more than the money invested, but only up to a certain point. After that, every dollar invested will be worth less than a dollar when the time comes to sell.

If you put $500 into minor fix-up and repair, you may see an extra $1,000 when you sell. On the other hand, if you pour $5,000 into improvement projects, you may only see a $2,000 increase in the selling price.

Watch your costs, and as you upgrade the property compare it with other houses in the same condition. Try to estimate how much impact your efforts are having on the real market value of your investment and quit while you're ahead.

MANAGING

If you want to keep the property and rent it out, be our guest. However, there are two considerations that you should take into account before you do so:

First, under current Federal tax laws you shouldn't invest in a rental property with negative cash flow—that is, where the money going out each month is less than the rental income. If you can't make money every month from the rental income, consider selling.

Second, until you've been a property manager you can't imagine the nightmare of answering the phone at 3 a.m. and finding out that you have an emergency. You don't know how deeply landlords hate deadbeats until one sneaks out of your rental house in the middle of the night.

We have chosen not to become landlords. We may, on occasion, allow the previous owners to remain as renters under an agreement called a *sale-leaseback*, but only in exceptional situations. Our goal is to buy property and have it back on the market within days.

There are many well-written books on the subject. If you want to keep your property, rather than sell it and jump back into the game again, buy a landlording primer and enjoy.

SELLING

We come at last to the last step on our uphill climb towards wealth: selling the property.

Steve Martin, the comedian, once claimed he had written a book: "How I Turned a Million Dollars in Real Estate into $25 Cash." His point was valid. Having a healthy equity on paper isn't the same as having a fat bank account and a thick wallet. You can't eat equity.

The first step in selling takes place long before the closing. It occurs way back when you are first investigating a property. Remember the quick-sale value? That's the price you know the property will sell for if you have to sell it quickly. You should have used that figure in your planning, not the property's full market value. Much of what you'll do at this point you should have taken into account all the way back when you were planning your offer.

The second step also took place long before the closing, when you were structuring the offer. You can only give as good as you get. If you assumed a high-interest loan, or one with severe qualifying restrictions, you can have little hope of finding a buyer tomorrow. If you ignored the warning to stay away from mortgages with due-on-sale clauses, or if you found one and failed to work out terms with the lender, you will find *yourself* foreclosed on.

If, however, you have structured the deal in such a way that you can sell the property below its full market value and still make a profit, you will make money in real estate. Then, and only then, you are ready to sell your property.

Using a Realtor

There's no written or unwritten law that says you must sell through a Realtor. You can do it alone, and we often do. However, there's a lot to be said for having someone else do the legwork, particularly the first time you sell.

On the negative side, you'll have to pay a commission. The long-standing tradition is a 6% commission (that is, 6% of the selling price), which will mean $4,800 cash on an $80,000 sale. That could cut rather deeply into anticipated profits.

In our case study (remember Gus and Doreen?) there was enough difference between our purchase price and our selling price to easily pay the commission, so we were happy to turn the task of selling over to a professional. As long as you've taken the commission into account and you can still make money, save yourself the time, expense, and bother. The buyer will, in effect, foot the bill, and you can put the rest in your pocket.

On the positive side, a good Realtor will actively sell the property. She will have the Multiple Listing Service advertise it, allowing every agent in town to act as your personal sales agent. If you've priced it below market value it won't take long to sell, by definition. (If it does take long to sell, you overestimated market value.)

Your Realtor will also be the one who puts up with all the paper work, guiding the buyer through the process of title search, escrow, and similar necessary details. Furthermore, your Realtor will be working for you and will act as a go-between for you and the buyer. The extra insulation can make your life much easier.

If there is enough equity to afford another percentage point, offer to pay a 7% commission. The extra point on an $80,000 sale means another $800, and that 7% waves a red flag in front of every Realtor in town. Now you have a highly motivated sales force, working like crazy to sell a property that is already listed below market value.

If that doesn't sell it within a month, you've seriously

overestimated the market value. Go back to square one and try again.

Selling Without an Agent

You may be somewhat skeptical about your ability to sell a home. After all, the previous owners may have tried desperately to sell for four months before you finally bought it for almost nothing. What makes you think you'll fare any better?

The problem isn't with you; it's with the previous owner. They sold out to you in the final days before the sale out of total desperation. If the home had been advertised at its quick-sale price, it would have sold months ago. Homeowners can get greedy, even when they are facing foreclosure. They are so caught up in what they think their home is worth, they forget what they paid for it. Before you sell, ask yourself a couple of questions:

What are potential buyers looking for, and how are they looking for properties? They are looking for good deals— houses selling below market value, with good terms and low down payments. And they are looking for them by reading the classified ads and talking to Realtors. Doesn't that simplify looking for buyers?

First, offer the house at a price somewhere between its full value and its quick-sale value. If at this point there is any question as to the property's market value, that is, if you haven't had an appraisal done, you can have one done now.

By offering a discount below the full market value, you will be attracting more buyers. An advertisement that claims you are willing to sell "20% below market value" is a sure winner. Also, by making the asking price higher than the price you are willing to settle for, you are leaving yourself some negotiating range. But there is always the possibility that you'll get your asking price.

Classified ads, "For Sale by Owner," are an unending source of buyers. A well-worded ad will cause your phone to ring off the wall. Put yourself in the buyers' shoes. What will they find attractive? A hint of desperation on your part will help:

> *Owner desperate—must sell now.*
> *Appraised $80,000, asking $69,000*
> *FHA 9% assumable loan. Call 555-2342*

Let your buyer "steal" your home from you. If there is $15,000 equity, why not share it with the next owner and walk away with $10,000?

Nothing Down Selling

One way to sell is by selling for nothing down—and still put money in your pocket! The problem most buyers face— the one you faced when you were shopping for property—is a lack of cash. If you ended up putting $10,000 into a property, you can't very well sell it for nothing down, can you? Or can you?

The answer involves creative financing and creative thinking. To illustrate this technique, we'll use another example.

You buy a home appraised at $100,000 for only $70,000, paying a total of $10,000 cash to reinstate the loan, pay the closing costs, and give the owners something for their equity. You have equity of $30,000, which you could probably sell for $20,000, recovering your $10,000 investment and taking the other $10,000 on a note. But you could sell it even faster if you offered to sell for nothing down, couldn't you?

You advertise a nothing-down deal, and nothing-down seminar graduates swarm like moths to a light bulb. They have learned one important thing: If you want to buy a

191

property with nothing down, you must meet the seller's price. That's important in this case because you must sell it for its full market value of $100,000. They have also learned to pledge their interest in other properties as part of their down payment, so you'll want to find an investor who is willing to do so.

There are two ways you can structure this deal:

1) First Method

$100,000	Sales price.
60,000	Assumption of first mortgage.
20,000	Second mortgage carried by you.
20,000	Mortgage against another property owned by the buyer, also carried by you. (Accept a first or second position only.)

The first and second mortgages must not exceed 80% of the property's market value. This rule also applies to the mortgage against your buyer's other property that you will hold. The interest rate on both mortgages should be as high as possible, and the length of the loan should be as short as possible—10 years is a good maximum.

You can take both of the mortgages you now own, with a total face value of $40,000, to a mortgage broker, who will pay cash for them. How much cash you receive will depend on several factors including the length of the term, what position they are in, the interest rate, and their loan-to-value ratio. In other words, the mortgage broker will pay you according to the return he expects to enjoy on those mortgages. You may get 50% or more of the face value of the mortgages; in this case, $20,000 cash—and you've doubled your money.

2) Second Method

$100,000	Sales price.
60,000	Assumption of first mortgage.
20,000	Second mortgage, carried by you.
20,000	Third mortgage, carried by you.

You could use this financing structure if the buyer didn't have another property on which you could hold a mortgage. You can still take the second mortgage and sell it to a mortgage broker, for $10,000 to $15,000 cash, recovering your original investment. The buyer would continue making payments to you on the third mortgage which you should record after you have sold your second mortgage.

You do have some risk in accepting a third mortgage on a property, especially when all of the equity is tied up in liens. However, analyzing your risk should put your fears to rest. If the buyer defaults on your mortgage, you can foreclose and take back the property, which you can then resell. If the buyer defaults on the first or the second, you can reinstate those loans and foreclose under the doctrine of endangered collateral.

Even if you chose not to take the property back, and allowed the first or second mortgage holder to foreclose and wipe out your third mortgage, you should have been able to sell your second for $15,000 or so, for a $5,000 profit. In any case, you're still money ahead.

Double Closing

If you find a buyer within your own escrow period (before you've bought the property yourself), you have two options: assign the contract (previously discussed), or a double closing.

The double closing involves two title transfers within a

relatively short period of time or simultaneously. For example, after you have signed a contract with the previous owner, you may find a buyer immediately to whom you can sell your property. Two deeds will be recorded: one from the previous owner to you, and one from you to the new buyer.

The real value in a double closing is the savings in title insurance. The search will have just been completed, so your buyer can pay for title insurance without having to conduct a title search, and you will have paid for a title search without having to buy insurance.

Wrap-around Mortgage

If you buy a property with little or no money down, and can afford to take your profit in payments, you may want to sell on a wrap-around mortgage (also called an all-inclusive trust deed or AITD). This is a contract that you, as a seller, create for your buyer. You do not allow the buyer to assume any existing mortgages; instead, you create a single new mortgage that "wraps around" the existing ones. Your buyer makes payments to you on your AITD and you continue making payments on the existing loans.

By asking only enough down payment to cover your own investment, you are able to recycle the same down payment again and again, each time taking your profit in monthly payments of about $100. If you buy 100 homes with this method, you still have your original down payment money and $10,000-a-month income for the next 20 years or so.

The wrap-around technique for investing is another example of proper prior planning. It can be an excellent source of turning real estate into a gold mine—if you plan your sale before you buy.

Our last word of advice on selling is a suggestion that you should follow before you ever buy the property. No matter what techniques you use, whether you sell through an agent or on your own, plan ahead. Use the accompanying form to anticipate actual selling costs. Too many investors think that the selling price is somehow directly related to their net proceeds from the sale. The two are really only third cousins by a second marriage.

If you bought the property from the owners you no doubt remember all the charges they had to pay at closing. Well, the shoe's on the other foot now. You'll be the one paying the seller's costs. If your buyers use FHA or VA financing, you'll even have to pay part of their points for them. Ask your banker for details. In some states the seller pays for the title search. In others it's the buyer's responsibility.

You will already be familiar with the costs, and your local title officer, banker, Realtor, and attorney can help you estimate them more precisely.

Actual Sale Proceeds

Selling Price	$_____
Less:	
Appraisal fee (optional)	_____
Realtor's commission (optional)	_____
Attorney's fees or title officer	_____
FHA or VA points (possibly)	_____
Prorated taxes	_____
Survey costs	_____
Title search and insurance	_____
Transfer taxes	_____
Other costs, as estimated	_____
Actual Proceeds from Sale	$_____

After you've taken everything into account subtract another $1,000 or so for Murphy's Law before you count your chickens—and even then don't spend it until it's in the bank.

The form is similar to the one you used when you planned your offer long ago. You'll want to do the same calculations again before you list the property for sale, just to be sure the numbers still add up to that same glorious return.

DO IT AGAIN

Oh, this is fun now, isn't it? You take your $10,000 cash profit, reward yourself with a weekend in the tropics, buy a new stereo, a small wardrobe—

Wait a minute. If you want more than a quick buck here and there—if your goal is to be really rich—may we suggest the following long-range plan, guaranteed to satisfy your every hedonistic craving?

Take 10% of your profit and reward yourself, and reinvest 90%. In doing so you will be able to increase your net profit exponentially. Compounding your profits always will do you better than spending them.

Anyone—and that definitely includes you—can become a millionaire within 5 to 10 years investing in foreclosure properties. Out of the hundreds of students we have taught in seminars and workshops, we have never had one who absolutely couldn't succeed if he or she was willing to try.

It takes time, persistence, and self-control when that first big check hits the bank. But if you're willing to do the work and follow the plan, there's no reason in the world you can't achieve any financial goal you set.

CONCLUSION

Right now, you should have the basis for locating, analyzing, buying and selling properties in distress. You may want a guarantee at this point. OK, here are your guarantees:

1) If you stay home and watch TV, you will not find any good deals.

2) If you never make a written offer, you will never buy real estate.

3) If you work the system, the system will work.

Your success is up to you. You are your own greatest competition. Every day, across the country, homeowners receive their notices of default. They read them with shaky hands and wish someone would help them out. Some of those homeowners will be lucky; they will come up with the money to save the mortgage or sell their homes for full market value. Others will be saved by an investor—a foreclosure expert— who may not give them the full market price for their homes, but who will save their credit and help them move ahead. Most of them, however, will lose their homes—voluntarily or by force—and you could have been there.

Get involved today. Assemble your team of experts. Make calls and visits. Stop by the county courthouse and spend an afternoon learning your way around. There are no real short-cuts to success, but there are some freeways with very high speed limits.

Appendix

The following table lists only the predominant method of foreclosure in each state. Some states, such as Arizona, have many other methods other than the one listed here. For instance, in Colorado if agricultural real estate is being fore-closed, then the redemption period is six months, as opposed to the more typical 75 days. Further, if the trust deed (or mortgage) was executed prior to July 1, 1965, there is also a six-month right of redemption. As you can see, you may have to research the law of your state for more detailed information than is provided in the table.

Foreclosure Summary State by State

State	Predominant Security Document	Predominant Foreclosure Method	Redemption Period	Possession During Redemption	Law Citation
Alabama	Mortgage	Power of Sale	12 mos.	Purchaser	Code of Alabama, Vol. 5, Title 6, Sections 6-5-240 et seq.; Vol. 19, Title 35-10-1 et seq.
Alaska	Trust Deed	Power of Sale	None		Alaska Statutes, Vol. 2, Title 9, Sections 09.45.170 et seq.; Title 34, Sections 34.20.070 et seq.
Arizona	Trust Deed	Power of Sale	None		Revised Statutes Annotated, Vol. 4A, Title 12; Vol. 11, Title 33, Sections 33-721 et seq.; 33-807 et seq.
Arkansas	Mortgage	Power of Sale	12 mos.	Purchaser	Arkansas Statutes Annotated, Vol. 5, Sections 51-1105 et seq.; Vol. 7B, Section 84-1201
California	Trust Deed	Power of Sale	None		California Civil Code Sections 2920 et seq., 2945 et seq.
Colorado	Trust Deed	Power of Sale	75 days	Mortgagor	Colorado Revised Statutes 1973, Vol. 16A, Title 38, Sections 38-37-101 et seq., 38-38-101 et seq., 38-39-101 et seq.
Connecticut	Mortgage	Strict Foreclosure	None	Purchaser	Connecticut General Statutes Annotated, Vol. 22A, Section 49-14, 49-17 et seq.
Delaware	Mortgage	Judicial	None		Delaware Annotated, Vol. 6, Sections 10-4716; 10-4961 et seq., 10-5061 et seq.

State	Predominant Security Document	Predominant Foreclosure Method	Redemption Period	Possession During Redemption	Law Citation
Florida	Mortgage	Judicial	10 days	Mortgagor	Florida Statutes Annotated Vol. 2, Section 435.031; Vol. 20, Section 702.01
Georgia	Security Deed	Power of Sale	None	Purchaser	Georgia Code Annotated, Book 20, Sections 67-115 et seq., 67-201, 67-401, 67-701, 67-1503 et seq.
Hawaii	Trust Deed	Power of Sale	None		Hawaii Revised Statutes, Vol. 7A, Sections 667-1 et seq.
Idaho	Trust Deed	Power of Sale	None		Idaho Code, Vol. 2, Sections 5-226 et seq., 6-101, 11-301, et seq., 11-401
Illinois	Mortgage	Judicial	6 mos.	Mortgagor	Illinois Code of Civil Procedure, Sections 12-122 et seq., 15-101 et seq.
Indiana	Mortgage	Judicial	12 mos.	Mortgagor	Burns' Indiana Statutes Annotated, Sections 32-8-11-2 et seq., 32-8-16-1, 32-8-17-1, 34-1-39-4 et seq., 34-2-29-3
Iowa	Mortgage	Judicial	6 mos.	Mortgagor	Iowa Code Annotated, Vol. 50, Sections 628.2 et seq., 654.1
Kansas	Mortgage	Judicial	12 mos.	Mortgagor	Kansas Statutes Annotated Vol. 4, Sections 58-2253 et seq.; Vol. 4A, Sections 60-2410 et seq.
Kentucky	Mortgage	Judicial	None	Mortgagor	Baldwin's Kentucky Revised Statutes, Vol. 7, Sections 426.200 et seq.
Louisiana	Mortgage	Judicial	None		Louisiana Revised Statutes Vol. 6, Article 2343; Vol. 10, Article 2568 Code of Civil Procedure; Vol. 7 4106, 4341 et seq., Vol. 8 4942 et seq.

State	Predominant Security Document	Predominant Foreclosure Method	Redemption Period	Possession During Redemption	Law Citation
Maine	Mortgage	Entry and Possession	12 mos.	Mortgagor	Maine Revised Statutes Annotated, Vol. 7, Sections 14-2151, 14-2202 et seq., 14-2251 et seq.; Vol. 8, Sections 14-6201 et seq.
Maryland	Trust Deed	Power of Sale	None		Annotated Code of Maryland, Vol. 9C, Rule W70 et seq., BR6
Massachusetts	Mortgage	Power of Sale	None		Annotated Laws of Massachusetts, Chapter 244, Sections 244-1 et seq., 244-17A, 244-35
Michigan	Mortgage	Power of Sale	12 mos.	Mortgagor	Michigan Statutes Annotated, Vol. 22, Sections 27A.3140, 27A.3201 et seq.
Minnesota	Mortgage	Power of Sale	6 mos.	Mortgagor	Minnesota Statutes Annotated, Vol. 37, Section 580.02 et seq., 581.10, 582.14 et seq.
Mississippi	Trust Deed	Power of Sale	None		Mississippi Code 1972 Annotated, Vol. 5, Sections 15-1-19 et seq.; Vol. 19, Sections 89-1-53 et seq.
Missouri	Trust Deed	Power of Sale	12 mos.	Mortgagor	Vernon's Annotated Missouri Statutes, Vol. 23, Sections 443.290 et seq.
Montana	Mortgage	Judicial	12 mos.	Mortgagor	Montana Code Annotated 1981, Vol. 3, Sections 25-13-801 et seq.
Nebraska	Mortgage	Judicial	None		Revised Statutes of Nebraska, Vol. 2, Sections 25-1530; 25-2137 et seq.

202

State	Predominant Security Document	Predominant Foreclosure Method	Redemption Period	Possession During Redemption	Law Citation
Nevada	Mortgage	Power of Sale	None		Nevada Revised Statutes, Vol. 2, Sections 21.130 et seq.; Vol. 3, Section 40.430; Vol. 5, Sections 106.025, 107.080 et seq.
New Hampshire	Mortgage	Power of Sale	12 mos.	Purchaser	New Hampshire Revised Statutes Annotated, Vol. 4A, Sections 479.19 et seq., Vol. 5, Section 529.26
New Jersey	Mortgage	Judicial	10 days		New Jersey Statutes Annotated
New Mexico	Mortgage	Judicial	10 mos.	Purchaser	New Mexico Statutes 1978 Annotated, Vol. 6, Sections 39-5-1, 39-5-19 et seq.; Vol. 7, Sections 48-3-14. 48-7-7
New York	Mortgage	Judicial	None		McKinney's Consolidated Laws of New York Annotated; Book 49 1/2, Sections 1352, 1401 et seq.
North Carolina	Trust Deed	Power of Sale	None		General Statutes of North Carolina, Vol. 1, Section 1-47; Vol. 2A, Sections 45-21.1 et seq.
North Dakota	Mortgage	Judicial	12 mos.	Mortgagor	North Dakota Century Code Annotated, Vol. 5A, Sections 28-24-01 et seq.; Vol. 6, Sections 32-19-1, 32-19-18, Vol. 7, Sections 35-22-01 et seq.
Ohio	Mortgage	Judicial	None		Page's Ohio Revised Code Annotated, Title 23, Section 2323
Oklahoma	Mortgage	Judicial	None		Oklahoma Statutes Annotated, Sections 12-686, 12-764, 46-31 et seq., 46-301

State	Predominant Security Document	Predominant Foreclosure Method	Redemption Period	Possession During Redemption	Law Citation
Oregon	Trust Deed Mortgage	Power of Sale Power of Sale	None 12 mos.	Purchaser	Oregon Revised Statutes, Vol. 1, Sections 86-010, 86-710 et seq., 88-040 et seq.
Pennsylvania	Mortgage	Judicial	None		Purdons Pennsylvania Statutes Annotated, Title 72, Sections 403 et seq., 5971o
Rhode Island	Mortgage	Power of Sale	None		General Laws of Rhode Island, Vol. 6, Sections 34-23-1 et seq., 34-26-1 34-27-1 et seq.
South Carolina	Mortgage	Judicial	None		Code of Laws of South Carolina 1976, Vol. 7, Sections 15-39-640 et seq.; Vol. 10, Sections 29-3-10, 29-3-630 et seq.
South Dakota	Mortgage	Power of Sale	12 mos.	Mortgagor	South Dakota Codified Laws 1967, Vol. 6, Section 15-19-23; Vol. 7, Sections 21-48-1 et seq.; 21-52-2 et seq.
Tennessee	Trust Deed	Power of Sale	24 mos.	Purchaser	Tennessee Code Annotated Vol. 4, Sections 16-16-111, 21-1-803, 35-501 et seq.; Vol. 11A, 66-8-101
Texas	Trust Deed	Power of Sale	None		Vernon's Civil Statutes of State of Texas Annotated, Vol. 12, Title 56, Articles 3810, 3819 et seq.; 1982 Texas Rules of Court, Rule 309
Utah	Trust Deed	Judicial	6 mos.	Mortgagor	Utah Code Annotated 1953 (1977), Vol. 9A, Sections 78-37-1, 78-40-8; Vol. 9B, Rules of Civil Procedure 69(e)1-3, 69(f)1-5

State	Predominant Security Document	Predominant Foreclosure Method	Redemption Period	Possession During Redemption	Law Citation
Vermont	Mortgage	Strict Foreclosure	6 mos.	Mortgagor	Vermont Statutes Annotated, Title 12, Sections 12-4529 et seq.; Rules of Civil and Appellate Procedure 80.1 (e)(h)
Virginia	Trust Deed	Power of Sale	None		Code of Virginia, Vol. 8, Sections 55-59 et seq.
Washington	Mortgage	Judicial	12 mos.	Purchaser	Revised Code of Washington Annotated, Title 6, Sections 6.24.010 et seq.; Title 61, Section 61.12.060
West Virginia	Trust Deed	Power of Sale	None		West Virginia Code, Vol. 11, Sections 38-1-1A et seq.; Vol. 16, Sections 59-3-1 et seq.
Wisconsin	Mortgage	Power of Sale	12 mos.	Mortgagor	West's Wisconsin Statutes Annotated, Section 815.31, 846.51 et seq.
Wyoming	Mortgage	Power of Sale	3 mos.	Mortgagor	Wyoming Statutes Annotated, Vol. 2, Sections 1-18-101 et seq.; Vol. 7, Sections 34-4-102 et seq.

State and National
Newspaper Associations

Here is list of organizations across the United States (and a few in Canada, too) from which you can obtain a directory listing all of the newspapers in your state publishing legal notices. Many times the most profitable deals are posted in some of the most obscure newspapers. Therefore, it is extremely advantageous for an investor to know what publications are available in his area to make locating those deals that much easier.

Alabama Press Assn.
Box 1800
Tuscaloosa, AL 35403
(205) 354-5611

Alaska Publishers Assn.
Box 1588
Juneau, AK

Allied Daily Newspapers
Box 11128
Tacoma, WA 98411-0128
(206) 272-3611

American Newspaper Publishers Assn.
Box 17407
Dulles International Airport
Washington, D.C. 20041
(703) 620-9500

Arizona Newspapers Assn.
4717 North Central Ave.
Phoenix, AZ 85012
(602) 277-3600

Arkansas Press Assn.
1701 Broadway
Little Rock, AR 72206
(501) 374-1500

California Newspaper Publishers Assn.
1127 11th St. Room 1040
Sacramento, CA 95814
(916) 443-5991

Canadian Daily Newspaper Publishers Assn.
321 Bloor St. E, Suite 214
Toronto, Ontario M4W1E7
CANADA
(416) 923-3567

Canadian Community Newspaper Assn.
705-88 University Avenue
Toronto, Ontario M5J1T6
CANADA
(416) 598-4277

Colorado Press Assn.
1336 Glenarm Place
Denver, CO 80204
(303) 571-5117

Connecticut Editorial Assn.
c/o Ronald Bartizer
Lakeville Journal
Box 353
Lakeville, CT 06039
(203) 435-9873

Florida Press Assn.
306 South Duval, Room 204
Tallahassee, FL 32301
(904) 222-5790

Georgia Press Assn.
1075 Spring St.
N.W. Alanta, GA 30309
(404) 872-2467

Hawaii Newspaper Publishers Assn.
c/o Catholic Herald
Honolulu, HA 96813
(808) 536-5495

Idaho Newspaper Assn.
Box 1067
Boise, ID 83701
(208) 343-1671

Illinois Press Assn.
929 South 2nd Street
Springfield, IL 62704
(217) 523-5092

(Indiana) Hoosier State Press Assn.
300 Consolidated Bldg.
115 N. Pennsylvania St.
Indianapolis, IN 46204
(317) 637-3966

Inland Daily Press Assn.
840 N. Lakeshore Drive
Suite 802 W
Chicago, IL 60611
(312) 440-1230

Iowa Newspaper Assn.
319 East 5th
Des Moines, IA 50309
(515) 244-2145

Kansas Press Assn.
Box 1773
Topeka, KA 66601
(913) 233-7421

Kentuckty Press Assn.
332 Capitol Avenue
Frankfort, KY 40601
(502) 223-8821

Louisiana Press Assn.
680 N. Fifth
Baton Rouge, LA 70802
(504) 344-9309

Maine Press Assn.
c/o James Thompson
Brunswick Times Record
Industry Road
Brunswick, ME 04011
(207) 729-3311

Maryland-Delaware-D.C. Press Assn.
College of Journalism
University of Maryland
College Park, MD 20742
(301) 837-6070

Massachusetts Press Assn.
c/o Robert Finneran
Andover Townsman
Box AT
Andover, MA 01810
(617) 475-1943

Michigan Press Assn.
827 North Washington Ave.
Lansing, MI 48906
(517) 372-2424

Minnesota Newspaper Assn.
84 South 6th St.
Minneapolis, MN 55402
(612) 332-8844

Mississippi Press Assn.
2720 N. State St.
Jackson, MS 39216
(601) 981-3060

Missouri Press Assn.
Eighth and Locust
Columbia, MO 65201
(314) 449-4167

Montana Press Assn.
1900 North Main Street
Suite C
Helena, MT 59601
(406) 443-2850

National Newspaper Assn.
1627 K Street NW
Suite 400
Washington, D.C. 20006
(202) 466-7200

National Newspaper Publishers Assn.
770 National Press Bldg.
Washington, D.C. 20045
(202) 638-4473

Nebraska Press Assn.
206 South 13th Street
Suite 723
Lincoln, NB 68508
(402) 476-2851

Nevada State Press Assn.
Box 137
Carson City, NV 89702
(702) 882-8772

New England Newspaper Assn.
70 Washington Street
Salem, MA 01970
(617) 744-8940

New England Press Assn.
Northeastern University
360 Huntington Ave.
Boston, MA 02115
(617) 437-2896

New Hampshire Press Assn.
c/o Doug Rooks
Granite State News
Wolfeboro, NY 03894
(603) 569-3126

New Jersey Press Assn.
206 W. State St.
Trenton, NJ 08608
(609) 695-3366

Publishers Bureau of New Jersey
2040 Millburn Ave.
Maplewood, NJ 07040
(201) 762-8080

New Mexico Press Assn.
Box 11278
Albuquerque, NM 87192
(505) 299-6143

New York Press Assn.
106 Pickard Drive
Syracuse, NY 13211
(315) 455-7403

New York State Publishers Assn.
11 N. Peral St.
Suite 1207
Albany, NY 12207
(518) 449-1667

North Carolina Press Assn.
Box 2019
Raleigh, NC 27602
(919) 821-1435

North Dakota Newspaper Assn.
Box 8137
University Station
Grand Forks, ND 58202
(701) 777-2574

Northwest Daily Press Assn.
84 South 6th St.
Suite 430
Minneapolis, MN 55402
(612) 338-7128

Ohio Newspaper Assn.
145 E. Rich St.
Columbus, OH 43215
(614) 224-1648

Oklahoma Press Assn.
3601 N. Lincoln
Oklahoma City, OK 73105
(405) 524-4421

Ontario Community Newspaper Assn.
Box 451
Oakville, Ontario L6J5A8
CANADA
(416) 844-0184

Oregon Newspaper Publishers Assn.
7150 SW Hampton St.
Suite 232
Portland, OR 97223
(503) 684-1942

Pennsylvania Newspaper Publishers Assn.
2717 North Front
Harrisburg, PA 17110
(717) 234-4067

Rhode Island Press Assn.
c/o Lenard Panaggio
Chatelet, Old Beach Road
Newport, RI 02840

South Carolina Press Assn.
Box 11429
Columbia, SC 29211
(803) 254-1607

South Dakota Press Assn.
Box 2230
Brookings, SD 57007
(605) 692-4300

Southern Newspaper Publishers Assn.
Box 28875
Atlanta, GA 30328
(404) 256-0444

Suburban Newspapers of America
111 E. Wacker Dr.
Chicago, IL 60601
(312) 644-6610

Tennessee Press Assn.
Box 8123
Knoxville, TN 37996
(615) 974-5481

Texas Daily Newspaper Assn.
3701 Kirby Dr.
Suite 1110
Houston, TX 77098
(713) 529-3531

Texas Press Assn.
718 West Fifth St.
Austin, TX 78701
(512) 477-6755

Utah Press Assn.
467 East 3rd South
Salt Lake City, UT 84111
(801) 328-8678

Vermont Press Assn.
c/o Mike Donoghue
Burlington Free Press
191 College St.
Burlington, VT 05401
(802) 863-3441

Virginia Press Assn.
300 West Franklin Street
Suite 101E
Richmond, VA 23220
(804) 648-8948

Washington Newspaper Publishers Assn.
3838 Stone Way North
Seattle, WA 98103
(206) 634-3838

West Virginia Press Assn.
Suite 203
1033 Quarrier Street
Charleston, WV 25301
(304) 342-1011

Wisconsin Newspaper Assn.
Box 5580
Madison, WI 53705
(608) 238-7171

Wyoming Press Assn.
710 Garfield
Suite 248
Laramie, WY 82070
(307) 745-8144

Glossary

Abstract of Judgment. A brief summary of a judgment. When recorded, an abstract of judgment creates a lien upon real and personal property.

Abstract of Title. A summary of the title history to a particular piece of real property, from the time it became a part of the United States to the present.

Acceleration Clause. A provision in a trust deed note or mortgage that calls for the outstanding balance to be immediately due and payable under specified conditions, such as a default of payment.

Amortization. A fixed period of time by which a debt is prorated in order to determine what the periodic payments will be.

Annual Debt Service. The amount of money paid in a 12-month period toward a mortgage or trust deed.

Appraisal. An opinion as to the market value of property, given by an impartial, qualified person, as of a certain date.

Appreciation. An increase in the worth or value of a property due to economic or related causes, which may prove to be either temporary or permanent. Opposite of *depreciation.*

Assignment. The process whereby the interest, claim, right, or title in property is transferred from one person to another.

Beneficiary. The lender on a note and trust deed. The beneficiary lends money to a trustor, and title is placed in care of a trustee, with power of sale in the case of default. The trust is created for the benefit of the beneficiary. See also *Trustor* and *Trustee.*

Cash Flow. The net spendable income from an investment, determined by deducting all operating and fixed expenses from the gross income. If expenses exceed income, a negative cash flow results.

Cash Flow After Taxes. The net income from an investment after taking into consideration all tax ramifications as well as the normal expenses.

Deed. A written instrument by which the owner of real property conveys his or her title. There are several forms of deed, varying in the degree to which the owner warrants the deed against defects in title. See also *Special Warranty Deed; General Warranty Deed; Quit Claim Deed; Deed of Trust; Trustee's Deed; Gift Deed; Sheriff's Deed.*

Deed of Trust. An instrument used to create a mortgage lien by which the mortgagor conveys his or her title to a trustee, who holds it as security for the benefit of the note holder (the beneficiary). Also called a *Trust Deed*.

Default. Failure to discharge or perform a legally binding obligation or duty.

Depreciation. In real estate investment, an expense deduction for tax purposes taken over the period of ownership of income property.

Discount. The difference between the purchase price if you pay all cash or cash and terms. (Cash With Terms Price – All Cash Price = Discount)

Down Payment. The amount of the selling price paid at the beginning and not financed.

Due-on-Sale Clause. A clause in a trust deed or mortgage demanding payment in full on the outstanding balance upon sale or alienation of title.

Encumbrance (or Incumbrance). A lien or claim upon title to real property that diminishes the value of the property but does not prevent transfer of title.

Equity. The value that an owner has in his or her property over and above any mortgage indebtedness.

Fixed Rate Mortgage. A loan with an unchanging interest rate, amortized over a given period of time. The payment amount stays the same throughout the duration of the mortgage.

Foreclosure. The procedure by which property is sold to pay a debt for which the property was pledged.

General Warranty Deed (or Warranty Deed). A deed in which the grantor makes written guarantees against defects in title. This offers the greatest protection to the grantee.

Gift Deed. A deed used to convey the title as a gift.

Grantee. The purchaser of real estate. The person to whom title is granted under a deed of trust.

Grantor. The owner of title being granted under the terms of a deed.

Interest. A charge made by a lender for the use of money.

Investment. Money directed toward the purchase, improvement and development of an asset in expectation of income or profits.

Lien. A claim on property for the purpose of securing the payment of a debt or obligation.

Lienholder (or Lienor). One who holds a lien.

Loan to Value. The amount of mortgage on a property divided by the current market value of the property. It is expressed as a percentage.

Mortgage. A conditional pledge or transfer of real estate as security for the payment of debt. Also, the document creating a mortgage lien.

Mortgagee. The lender of money who accepts a mortgage from the borrower to secure a debt.

Mortgagor. The borrower of money who gives a mortgage to the lender as security for a debt.

Net Operating Income. The income after all fixed costs and operating expenses are deducted from the gross income.

Note (or Promissory Note). A written promise, signed by the borrower, to repay a certain sum to the lender. A promissory note will also contain the terms of repayment.

Principal. The original amount (as in a loan) of the total due and payable at a certain date. In a fully amortized loan, this is the portion of the payment that is not interest.

Promissory Note. See *Note.*

Quit Claim Deed. A deed in which the grantor conveys only such rights, title, and interest as he legally holds. This offers the least protection to the grantee of all deeds.

Real Property. That which is immovable, affixed to the land, including trees, buildings and permanent attachments to buildings.

Record. To incorporate into the written public record, giving notice of title, claim, or interest in real property.

Self-Liquidating. A loan that is amortized over a specific period of time and at the end of that period the loan is paid in full.

Sheriff's Deed. Similar to trustee's deed, but given by a court, rather than a trustee, pursuant to the sale of real property by the court.

Special Warranty Deed. A deed for real property in which the grantor warrants against only those liens and encumbrances during the time the grantor held title.

Straight Line Cost Recovery. A method of calculating depreciation for tax purposes, computed by dividing the adjusted basis of the property by the estimated number of years of remaining useful life. The length of time over which the property must be depreciated is set by the Internal Revenue Service and is currently 27.5 years.

Tax Bracket. The percentage of ordinary income taxed by the government. Under current Federal law, most taxpayers will pay either 15 percent or 28 percent of their income in taxes, depending on their taxable income.

Tax Lien. A lien held by the state or federal government against real or personal property, for delinquent taxes.

Trustee. The party in a trust deed who holds legal title without having beneficial title, with power of sale in case of default by the trustor. See also *Trustor* and *Beneficiary.*

Trustee's Deed. A deed of conveyance executed by a trustee pursuant to a trustee's sale.

Trustee's Sale. A public sale or auction conducted by a trustee on behalf of a beneficiary, under the powers of sale contained in a trust deed.

Trustor. The borrower under a trust deed and note. The trustor enjoys beneficial title but no legal title until the note is paid in full. See also *Trustee* and *Beneficiary.*

Variable Rate Mortgage. A mortgage loan in which the interest rate may increase or decrease at specified intervals, within certain limits based on a specified economic indicator.

Warranty Deed. See also *General Warranty Deed.*

Index